1

Introduction: Is Intellectual Capital a "New Big Idea"?

BIG IDEAS

The "big idea" is as much a part of business folklore as the "home run" is of American culture. We commonly speak of our insights as though they could be ranked on a scale from small to large: good ideas, fresh ideas, bright ideas, brilliant ideas, sensational ideas, breakthroughs, master strokes, blockbusters, ideas of a lifetime, and finally home runs and grand slams.

In business, furthermore, we speak of product ideas, engineering ideas, financing ideas, organizational ideas, promotional ideas, marketing ideas, management ideas, and many more—each functional category being additionally divisible from small to large.

What is most preferred in business, compared to all other ideas, is "the big idea that makes a million." And while it cannot be denied that such ideas occasionally do occur, they are very rare. Business routinely operates much more on singles, bunts, and sacrifices than on home runs. Despite this reality, however, business searches relentlessly for "new big ideas" and "magic

3

answers," which will remove the need to plod along, day by day, one small idea at a time, and worker by worker.

At the risk of turning away readers who are hoping to find an easy way to become the next Babe Ruth of business ideas, let me be honest about what is offered here: This book is a collection of common sense ideas (mainly "small" rather than "big") that have helped me to enjoy business and to make a little more money for the companies in which I have worked, and for my own businesses. There are no guaranteed formulas, no "proven recipes for success," no "easy ten-step methods," and no buzzwords to impress your peers except the phrase "intellectual capital" itself.

VALUABLE IDEAS

When it comes to judging the value of ideas, there is one principal way that interests me more than any other—*whether they work.* In the framework of this book, the criterion by which ideas are judged is whether or not they work to make more money for the business enterprise of which you are a part. An idea is classed as a "valuable idea" if you can tell, after you have tried it, that it made money: either you have the positive results from testing it in the market or you have the conviction that it enabled you in some small way to outwit your competition. So we will not be concerned here with a theoretical or academic standard. The reader will decide which ideas in the book sound good enough to try, after which the proof is in the pudding.

Compared to the ideas of leading business consultants, which blare loudly from the covers of bestsellers (like *In Search of Excellence, Powerplay, Re-Inventing the Corporation, Thriving on Chaos, The Renewal Factor,* and many others), the ideas in this book are "quiet." If you are tired of pretending that big ideas come easy, if you know that profitable change comes in small, tough doses, then this book is for you. Take what you want and quietly try it.

✦

Ideas

The universal symbol for an "idea" is a light bulb. In the comics, a character will be seen brooding deep in thought in one frame, and smiling with insight in the next, with a light bulb flashing above his or her head. This symbol conveys the making of a connection in the mind, or what the biologist would call a neurological synapse. In more traditional terms, the symbol shows the light of the intellect at work, the immediacy with which insight can occur, and the power our thoughts have over our actions.

Ideas occur initially in rough or unprocessed form, like intellectual raw materials, and can be left as is or moved along into more complete or finished *concepts*. When we speak of the ideas of some great philosopher, we mean his or her serious, fully developed thought as it appears in his or her writings. In this sense, we can have "book-length ideas," which are a series of connected insights presented in a *context* that gives them life. When the connections between many such ideas are natural, strong, and easy to grasp, we speak of them as having *coherence*.

Single ideas can be held in the mind, at least momentarily, for evaluation. But no idea exists for long by itself, in surgical distinction. Every "new" idea depends on, and combines with, "old" ideas. A tiny new spark can trigger years of cumulative potential flame.

The recommendation in this chapter to "test an idea in the market" sounds easier than it is. "Bad" ideas can sometimes work if they are pursued aggressively enough. Furthermore, what works at first may not continue to work, and what works over the very long term is difficult to judge indeed.

INCREASED BUSINESS COMPETENCE: THE RESULT OF MORE INTELLECTUAL CAPITAL

Thousands of books have been written on how to succeed in business, and no one definition can be given for the concept of "business competence." However, we might agree that whatever competence is, it comes in different *degrees*. At any given moment, some businesspeople are simply much more competent than others. This conception of degree can illuminate the role of the intellect in overall competence, and the prevailing conditions in today's marketplace that put such a premium on intellectual growth.

Suppose we consider business competence as if it could be put on a simple scale of one to ten. A clerk on her first day of work is rated "1." A CEO in his prime is rated "10." In the context of such a scale, we can posit the following "law":

> *Law of Evolving Competence.* If you are doing things right, and if your company is competitive, then your business competence is always (at least) one notch lower than what your job seems to require.

For example, if you are a "6" on the scale of competence, then you will find yourself working in a job requiring a "7." As your competence improves and you grow in ability to a "7," you will be promoted to a job requiring an "8." You will never possess sufficient competence to have the feeling that you really know what you are doing. If you do, the company for which you work is about to become uncompetitive.

CEOs with a competence rating of "10" also find themselves insufficient. The market in which their companies are struggling to survive—especially in the slow-growth, hypercompetitive American markets of today—demand of them a performance of "11," which is off the scale.

An individual who goes from a competence rating of "6" to a new rating of "7" has acquired what I call a new amount of "intellectual capital." The use of this term is stylistic. I hope to draw the reader's attention away from the extrasomatic concept of monetary capital to the mental source of wealth, which is surely our intelligence and the ability to use it fully. I submit that just as a business has a "capital assets sheet," it should also have a recognition of its "intellectual capital." In the coming decade, banking capital will not be of greater importance to the firm than intellectual capital.

How do you increase your competence? First of all, there are no shortcuts. Suppose you are a "6," working in a "7" job. You decide to hire a consultant to help you increase your competence. The consulting firm sends out two people, a "3" and a "4." This does not work; the total of the two junior people does not reach "7." You send them back and you ask for a single person who is already a "7." The consulting firm says it has such a person, but then it tells you the price. You cannot afford him or her. No one who is a "7" prices himself or herself right for a "6"; a "7" prices himself or herself as a "7" (or more), because that is the market.

The *one and only way* to increase business competence is as follows:

1. Try things,

2. Fail,

3. Learn,

4. Try again.

Two consequences of this method follow, one concerning the company and the other concerning the individual.

A company that does not provide a climate of support for the individual going through this process is about to become uncompetitive, in the same fashion as the firm just mentioned, which does not promote people somewhat ahead of their growth in competence. Many companies talk bravely about the need for "trial and error," when what they really demand is "success without failure." Certainly a company must have successes or it will fail; but the successes can only emerge from a context that permits the individual to fail, to learn, and to recover for another try. When the company achieves such a climate, this is the atmosphere that makes it worthwhile for the individual to risk the intense pain of personal growth.

EMOTION: THE CONSTANT BACKDROP FOR GROWTH OF INTELLECTUAL CAPITAL

The second consequence of the "one-and-only method" given for increasing business competence (i.e., acquiring additional kinds and quantities of intellectual capital) is that the individual business intellect has to function, much of the time, amidst deep emotions and fears of failure.

The fear of failure is strong. The ego does everything possible not to fail, and, afterwards, not to see that it has done so. The ego attempts to deny criticism, to escape reality, and to ignore negative results from the marketplace.

In business, failures are so hard to take that no one has the heart to analyze them or to understand in detail exactly what caused them. Firms do not seek a careful critique of disasters, in the sense of scholarly or "literary" criticism. It is easier and more pleasant to start over on something else, to look for a "new big idea" and to let the past alone. It is even easier to fire someone who can be blamed for the failure than to apply the intellect to the case, fact by fact and person by person, in an effort to increase not only individual but team competence.

In today's business culture, leaders are not supposed to fail. They are supposed to lead by knowing what to do, before they do it. Companies that follow this theory use what may be called a "Darwinian" process in selecting managers for promotion:

Those managers with high innate competence and a "hitting streak" are advanced until the streak runs out and those managers with merely solid competence and no hitting streak are left behind.

I do not dispute the practice of "finding the right person for the problem," or, conversely, "finding the right problem (or niche) for the person." But I think that these are too often excuses for changing the people instead of changing the mind.

Furthermore, I agree that top executive salaries are deservedly higher than other jobs, because top executives must have a knack for what they do—they *must* often have "hitting streaks," they *must* usually be righter, and they *must* usually not fail. But no executive can escape failure either occasionally or perhaps regularly. And at the other extreme, no executive can be completely reasonable about his or her successes. I claim that the most powerful resource available to us is an intellect that can function as an intellect precisely at those times when it is least likely to have a serene emotional setting.

Such an assertion is by no means new. It is, in fact, an old refrain: "If you can keep your head when all about you are losing theirs . . . ," or "Think and Grow Rich." An entirely new principle is not being offered here, but some small ideas about how to execute an old one. The ideas are mainly common sense, but because business has been preoccupied with a search for "higher magic," the ideas have surprising power.

COURAGE: THE DRIVER OF GROWTH IN INTELLECTUAL CAPITAL

As we have defined it, business competence is an aggregate made up of many simultaneous factors; your rating on the scale of one to ten is a composite. You will have an ace or two, along with your deuces. If you are a "6" working in a "7" job, there will be at least a few aspects of your performance deserving an

"8" or a "9." These abilities permit a toehold for your confidence while you find the courage to use the one and only true method of advancement: to try something, to fail, to learn, and to try again.

The use of brilliant ideas and sparkling intellect is not without courage. In business, courage is required first to put forward reason amidst emotional situations, as already mentioned, and second to put forward reason that is new to others, regardless of the situation. Courage is especially needed if the "new reason" is alien to the culture of the business at hand or irreverent to social institutions of the country in which the business is based.

I believe that the more realistic and rational you are, the easier it is to be courageous. I believe that American managers have trouble in this regard because they have been encouraged to see things in complex ways, rather than in plain ways. They have been encouraged to explain their world in trendy business jargon, rather than in plain English.

But full use of clarity does not relieve the need for raw courage, nor eliminate the associated condition in business called stress. To me, the notion of business without stress is like the idea of a universe without risk. Adding value to your surroundings requires taking actions for which the results cannot be forecast; if you *can* forecast your results, you will not compete with others attempting to do the same thing. Stress is the human condition accompanying operations of high risk, and it seems to me a completely natural property of the universe.

In other words, you are unlikely to have original, money-making ideas without stress because of competition. Competition means that someone (lots of someones) will be doing things that stress him or her; that is, he or she will be attempting things that may not work, in order to stay ahead of you. The things that are known to work, or that can easily be projected to work, have already all been tried. The things that remain to be tried are much more chancy and produce greater stress in the teams who try them.

ANOTHER KEY TO INTELLECTUAL CAPITAL: LEARNING HOW TO LEARN

Professor Neil Postman of New York University, author of the American critique *Amusing Ourselves to Death*, says, "The most important thing one learns is always something about how one learns." Most of the ideas in this book are in this vein, and deal with how to learn something rather than what things, "hard and fast," have already been learned.

A management consultant friend of mine, John Minor of Boston, once told me to keep a notebook divided page by page between "what works" and "what doesn't work." He said that I should make note of what does not work or be doomed to try it again. I have indeed kept such a notebook, but in going back over it, I find I have a much greater affinity for what does work than for what does not. Such will be the case in this book; mostly, the ideas have worked.

The ideas in this book have flowed from a single human mind, and in that sense they are coherent. This does not mean that some will not seem contradictory with others, or that many will not overlap. By and large, the ideas have occurred at specific moments in time, in response to particular business situations, and have been recorded on separate sheets of my "what works/what doesn't work" notebook. In other words, the ideas occurred mainly as units and the reader may take them this way. There is no reason not to take some and reject others. There is no overarching, integrated *system* to be found here but rather patches of illumination and ways to change attitudes. Some of these attitudes will fit with and enhance the intellectual capital you already have.

2

Who First Had the Idea of Intellectual Capital, and What Does It Mean?

Although nearly 40 years have passed, I remember a few odd things from my introductory course in philosophy at college, where we read Plato and Aristotle. I remember Plato's concept of Ideals (such as perfect beauty, truth, and justice), which we will come to later in this book, and Aristotle's methods of defining the causes of things. Aristotle used four kinds of causes and he recommended defining something by saying first what it *was* and second what it *was not*. Much later, I remember discovering that everything we attempt to define requires the development of appropriate and extensive *context*.

Thus, the job of this chapter is to say what intellectual capital is by means of giving its derivation and by means of listing and elaborating its main components. The job of the remaining six chapters in Part 1 of the book is to say what intellectual capital is not and to provide context for a better overall understanding. In order to do this I will compare my concept of intellectual capital with a journalistic notion of "business brainpower" (Chapter 3), with what one leading American scholar considers the "intellectual life" today (Chapter 4), with common ideas about what a college education should provide the intellect (Chapter 5), and with the less than logical way in which the modern world is actually organized (Chapter 6). Finally, I will emphasize the role of attitudes—the key component to enhancing intellectual capital, even though they are one of the most difficult things on earth to change (Chapter 7).

But first, let me try to say what intellectual capital *is*.

DERIVATION OF THE PHRASE, INTELLECTUAL CAPITAL

The word "capital" has been with us since the Middle Ages. It has been used by all the famous economists, who have often given it a special meaning in their theories. But no layperson has any real trouble knowing basically what the word means. In everyday speech, "capital" and "money" are synonymous.

More recently, we find the term *human capital*. This term has been used only for the past couple of decades. Human capital originates with American economist Theodore W. Schultz, who won the Nobel Prize in 1979. Schultz began his career as an agricultural economist who was interested in the progress of the world's poorest people. As his experience and research widened, Schultz began to argue that the traditional concepts of economics were inadequate for treating the growth prospects of low-income countries:

> The decisive factors of production in improving the welfare of poor people are not space, energy, and cropland; the decisive factors are the *improvement in population quality and advances in knowledge*. (Schultz, 1981, p. 4; italics added)

This is an argument with more natural appeal than the usual mathematical theories of economists. Schultz continues:

> Child care, home and work experience, the acquisition of information and skills through schooling, and other investments in

health and schooling can improve population quality. (Schultz, 1981, p. 7)

The term Schultz uses to capture this qualitative concept of economic growth is *human capital*. A rigorous definition of human capital is not within our reach, Schultz says, but he makes the following distinctions:

> Consider all human abilities to be either innate or acquired. Every person is born with a particular set of genes which determines his innate ability. . . . Attributes of acquired population quality, which are valuable and can be augmented by appropriate investment, will be treated as *human capital*. (Schultz, 1981, p. 21; italics added)

The acquisition of additional human capital is not free, according to Schultz. Human capital requires investment of physical resources and monetary capital. But in the twentieth century, especially in high-income countries, people have made human capital the top priority. In advanced countries:

> (1) The rate of return on investment in human capital has tended to exceed the rate of return on investment in physical capital;
>
> (2) The rate at which human capital increases exceeds that of non-human capital; and
>
> (3) The central issue is the increase in the economic value of human time. . . . This rise in the value of human time is, in large part, a consequence of the formation of new kinds of human capital in response to economic incentives. (Schultz, 1981, pp. 60, 74)

Schultz's concept of human capital has recently been elaborated further by Paul Romer, a professor at the University of California at Berkeley. In most economic theory, there are three main factors of production: land, labor, and capital. In Romer's view, we must add the factors of human capital (measured by years of education) and ideas (measured by numbers of patents).

The notion of human capital developed by Schultz and Romer is close to what we want in this book, but it is aimed at whole populations. What I seek to do here is to focus on the individual, and on the individual who is already highly educated. Thus, the term *human capital* is not quite right for our purpose.

A more appropriate term is *intellectual capital*. This term has also been around for a number of years, although it has not been treated in formal economic theory to the same extent as Schultz's human capital concept. The first use of *intellectual capital* I could find in the literature was by the economist John Kenneth Galbraith.[1] In a 1969 letter to the Polish economist and prolific writer, Michal Kalecki, Galbraith said:

> I wonder if you realize how much those of us the world around have owed to the intellectual capital you have provided over these past decades. (Feiwel, 1975, p. 17)

This usage comes much closer to what I am about to propose than Schultz's and Romer's human capital. The earlier concept fits well when we think of masses of people; the Galbraith letter to Kalecki is more individualized, and it concerns something more definitely cerebral; we must be careful not to lean too far in that direction either.

To be the most useful, the concept of intellectual capital must mean more than "intellect as pure intellect"; it must have a degree of "intellect in action." Michal Kalecki is a case of the former more than the latter. Kalecki contributed hundreds of articles to the literature of economic theory and political policy, and today he is credited with having anticipated John Maynard Keynes's *General Theory*. Keynes, on the other hand, was not only a writer but an actor in the economic and political drama

---

[1] A friend of mine, Dr. Paul Olscamp, president of Bowling Green State University, in reviewing this manuscript, told me that he first heard the term *intellectual capital* in his Economics 101 class by Professor Inman at Western Ontario University in 1956.

of his times, who served as British Chancellor of the Exchequer. Keynes not only had ideas, but also had the courage to speak out on them, the ability to convince other men of them, and, thus, the power to get them tested against reality. When Keynes came to the United States for the Bretton Woods monetary conference during World War II, he had more intellectual capital than anyone else in attendance; Keynes and his ideas thus had a powerful formative effect on the entire structure of postwar international finance.

DEFINITION OF THE TERM "INTELLECTUAL CAPITAL"

Business readers know, intuitively, why this book is being written and what they stand to gain. They know how much a continuing stream of good ideas can be worth to a business, and they know that markets are getting tougher and tougher with every passing year. Easy growth in business is extremely rare today. Markets, especially in the United States, are mature and often shrinking and the principal way to survive is to beat competition. What beating competition means, across all levels and functions of an organization, is being *smarter.*

So the goal of this book is to build intellectual capital. What is meant by intellectual capital is the combination of four factors:

1. Your genetic inheritance,

2. Your education,

3. Your experience, and

4. Your attitudes about life and business.

Each reader has a unique combination of these four factors. Whatever total intellectual capital you have is in fact *singular;* its structure is unique. Intellectual capital cannot be mass produced. But the singular structure you presently possess can be significantly enhanced.

Of the four factors, the one that most lends itself to change in mid-career, and, thus, to a more powerful overall structure of your intellectual capital, is your attitudes about life and business. This book is mainly a sharing of attitudes that have worked to build intellectual capital and those that have not, in the author's experience, along with creative challenges to your "attitudinal status quo" (taken mainly from the province of the humanities, which includes religion and philosophy, art and music, and literature and history).

The definition of an individual's intellectual capital can hardly stand apart from three further factors, which characterize the organization of which the individual is a part:

5. Systems,

6. Culture, and

7. Research.

An individual can have high intellectual capital, but if the organization has poor systems by which to track his or her actions (trials and errors), the overall intellectual capital will not be as great as it can be.

In addition, the culture of an organization must permit the individual to try things, to fail, to learn, and to try again. If the culture unduly penalizes failure, it will have a small amount of success. Furthermore, the culture of an organization, to maximize its intellectual capital, must be keenly interested in criticism; that is, criticism in the sense of scholarly or "literary" criticism. The organization must want to know exactly what has happened to it in the past—the near past as well as the distant past—whether this be success or failure, or in between.

The organization seeking its highest possible stock of intellectual capital must also have a genuine interest in research. It must have humility and curiosity about what it is doing rather than arrogance and militaristic direction. It must be willing to find out about the world as it is rather than as management *wants* it to be. It must accept the truth about markets, even when the news is bad. It need not necessarily spend billions on research, but what it spends must be directed squarely at truth and conducted with a high degree of "intellectual honesty."

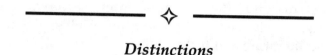

Distinctions

Our experience with the process of *definition* changes markedly from childhood to maturity, moving from easy linkages to more and more difficult *differences*.

In the first stage of this process, we simply link words with objects, as in the case of "apples" and "oranges." Next we link words with strings of other words, as in the case, say, of "triangle" (any figure with three straight sides).

The peak of ability with concrete definitions comes when we study geometry and algebra. An "equilateral triangle" is one having all three sides of equal length; we show by means of positing and proving a theorem that each angle of an equilateral triangle is exactly 60 degrees.

In early maturity, however, the arrogance that our command of language makes things easy begins to fade. Words, and strings of words, develop subtle differences. Solid concepts become slippery. Even "facts" themselves seem to have two or more interpretations.

In late maturity, the intellect pays a premium for more and more careful *distinctions*—not only those based on logical analysis of dissimilarities, but also those founded especially on experiential evidence and common sense. The adult mind is not built on a tightly integrated set of yes-no distinctions, but on a much looser amalgam of overlappings and contradictions. To enhance the structure of our knowledge thus requires a strong attitude of tolerance; we must not rush too fast to clean out the "junk" and to straighten every "mess" into an arrangement that is tidy but not productive.

3

Does Having More Intellectual Capital Mean Having More Information?

A universal complaint of all business executives is that they have too much information. The board members of a company complain of too much information to read before each meeting. The CEO of a company complains of too much information from his or her staff. The staff complains of too much information from the operating divisions, the accounting department, the market research group, outside consultants, government regulators, and many other sources.

Our time period has been labeled "The Age of Overinformation" by dozens of writers. And yet, despite this general recognition of its overabundance, nothing seems to happen, and the deluge of information continues and even accelerates.

The lament about too much information is ironic, inasmuch as those complaining most loudly are simultaneously worried about running *out* of everything, especially energy and raw materials. Of all the key raw materials we might name, information is the most crucial, both in itself and as the tool by which to find and more efficiently use other resources.

Let us distinguish roughly at this point between information and knowledge. Information is the raw material, and knowledge the finished product. By knowledge we mean "processed information," or that which can add value to the universe where before there was none. Although we witness every day a surplus of the raw material, we would by no means say that we had a surplus of the finished product. We would not agree that humanity has added "too much value" to the universe, but only too much information. Indeed, it is the premise of this book that a powerful need exists, and is growing, for more and more knowledge, or of what I have chosen to call intellectual capital.

Human life and the production of information have always been necessarily associated. The capacity to generate information increases with the age of a person and cumulatively with the age and growth of civilization, and so too increases the amount of genuine knowledge. But what is striking about the present period in time is the acceleration in the amount of the raw material without a similar rapid rise in the finished product. This is especially true about the more general kinds of knowledge, as opposed to the specialized. For instance, computer science is a special kind of knowledge that is growing very rapidly, indeed even more rapidly than the raw material (information) it enables.

Actually, the complaint about too much information is not made today in all *places* of the world, but mainly (if not only) in the advanced, democratic countries of the West. Until very recently, there was no surplus of information in the former Soviet Union, in fact just the opposite, and this leads us to the connection between plentiful information and freedom. At no time in history has a greater share of humanity or a larger absolute number of people lived in political freedom, and (consequently) at no time has there been a greater abundance of information, and also of knowledge, despite the fact that the raw material now seems to outpace the finished product.

The connection between abundant information and freedom is causal, but the link is not unidirectional. In other words,

━━━━━━━━━━ ◆ ━━━━━━━━━━

Information

Distinction Number 1

In the final act of *Macbeth*, the murderous king is surrounded and facing the end. After hearing news of his queen's death in another part of the castle, Macbeth says with dark sarcasm that she would have died sometime anyway, and he then makes the following defiant (and famous) speech about meaninglessness:

> Life's but a walking shadow, a poor player
> That struts and frets his hour upon the stage
> And then is heard no more. It is a tale
> Told by an idiot, full of the sound and fury,
> Signifying nothing.

Purely from the standpoint of the *science of information*, it makes no difference at all whether Macbeth's pessimistic view of the world is right or wrong. In other words, the electronic processes involved in transmitting a message composed by an idiot are identical with those involved in transmitting a message of great meaning, whether composed by Shakespeare or by Lincoln in his Gettysburg Address. The great advances of the past several decades have been in matching messages to transmitters, in encoding each message via elementary "bits," in reducing the signal-to-noise ratio of the transmission channel, in storing data and other signals for use later, and in decoding the message with high fidelity to its original pattern. These great advances are all completely independent of whether the message itself has any meaning.

The study of information as electronic signals is a science. The study of what information *means* is not. The intellect has as much trouble today determining which facts are really facts, and making a sound interpretation of a large body of such facts, with or without computers and the science of information.

Information

Distinction Number 2

Two or three centuries ago, people could speak of having "good" information about a subject, or at least "better" information about a business situation than their competitors. The "best" such information resided in trade and banking, where each firm posted trustworthy observers (often relatives) at key points around the world. The operation of this kind of network was expensive, and only a few other than traders and bankers could afford the price per message involved in this long-distance reporting. Partly because of this cost barrier, the information had high competitive value and easily paid for itself.

Consider the situation today, however, in which the science of information has sharply reduced the cost of transmitting and receiving messages. Today, the global electronic network reaches everywhere, and virtually all of us are both reporters and subscribers. The idea of good information, in the old sense, is obsolete; no one has better information about the sailing of cargoes, the prices of stocks, or any other variety of world events than anyone else. For a nominal sum, any businessperson who wishes can have all the news and commercial information he or she wants, immediately, every minute of every hour.

The problem today is not mainly in determining the *meaning* of a pattern of data or a body of facts, as was the case in centuries past. The problem today is much more a matter of deciding which channels of information to turn on or which to turn off because the surplus of available information will quickly inundate even the most energetic observer. To ignore the need for making such decisions, especially to turn some sources *off,* and to continue the futile struggle to "digest everything," is the worst possible mistake of all. Getting "more information" on an uncertain subject is no guarantee of finding knowledge. Greater intellectual capital follows not only from wisely limiting one's information sources, but also from the freeing of time from information "gathering" to information "processing."

information feeds on freedom and vice versa, but it is hard to say which comes first.

For example, consider the timing of the collapse of communism. It is easy now to say that the Berlin Wall could not have stood forever and that, in fact, it had been ready to fall for a long time. But the intriguing question remains, why did it happen in 1989, and not, say, in 1979 or 1983?

One obvious factor, of course, was the emergence in the mid-1980s of a certain Mikhail Gorbachev as leader of the Soviet Union and his policy of *glasnost*, which permitted more openness of information. But how different was Gorbachev's approach from what would have been pursued by *any* other Soviet leader of his generation?

I first heard the "Gorbachev has no choice" argument in 1987 from Dr. S. Frederick Starr, president of Oberlin College and a professor of Soviet history. Starr said in a speech that Gorbachev was helpless to do anything different from the "open information" approach, because information itself was rapidly becoming the central raw material of all economic activity. *Not only could the Supreme Soviet no longer keep information out of the USSR, but the Soviet government must actively open the way for a greater and greater flow of information—or face economic decline.* These political consequences were due to the underlying trend in electronic technology to make bits of information cheaper and cheaper and to the freedom in the West to let information flow anywhere it will.

So for Gorbachev to "ride the fundamentals," Starr said, and to save the Soviet economy, he had no choice but to seek a policy of freedom of information and to permit individual incentives in place of rigid central plans.

Data on the cost of computer information storage gives striking support to Starr's thesis on the timing of communism's collapse. Figure 3–1 shows the "information power of a dollar," which is the amount of "hard drive" computer storage you can buy with one dollar and which is, in turn, indicative of the cost of all kinds of information. Information power, so defined,

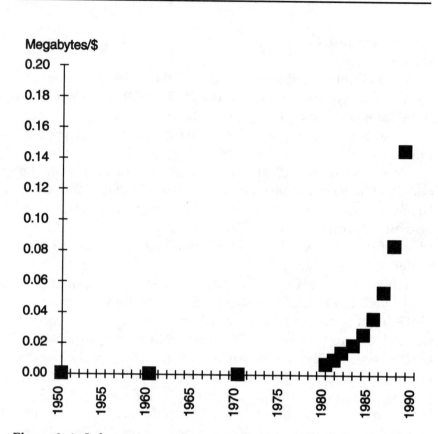

Figure 3–1 Information power per dollar (megabytes of computer storage available per dollar of expenditure), 1950–1990. In the period since World War II, the availability of humankind's key resource, information, is moving literally off the scale.

shows only a slight gain for three postwar decades, but then explodes. Growth is almost imperceptible on the graph between 1950 and 1980—though during these three decades we were actually quite amazed by the progress.

But look what happens in the 1980s. As computers get significantly bigger, faster, more friendly, and cheaper, the information power per dollar literally goes "off the scale." Eventually, the growth in information power may slow down, but we have as of now no means to say when such a deceleration might begin. Whole new families of information technology are announced routinely, such as experiments showing that a computer can be made entirely of light signals (via linked lasers), eventually offering processing speeds a thousand times faster than today's. The growth curve now points straight up through the 1990s and beyond. The curve is hard to taper mathematically without extending it several decades, perhaps to the year 2020 or beyond, as shown in Figure 3–2.

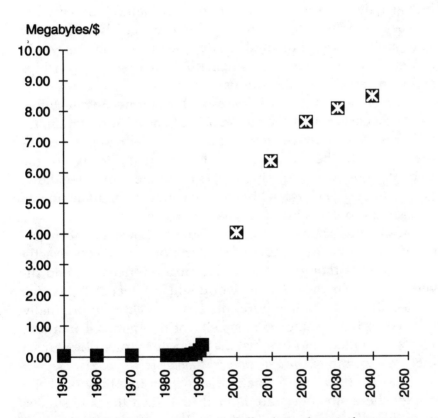

Figure 3–2 Information power per dollar (megabytes of computer storage available per dollar of expenditure), 1950–2050. Maybe, by the year 2020, some gradual deceleration may occur in information power, but, if so, at between 50 and 100 times more power than today.

As stated earlier, in today's world the abundance of knowledge trails the abundance of information, but I have also just demonstrated that this is not true across all disciplines. Technical knowledge of information itself—how to produce it electronically, store it, and transmit it—is clearly in abundance. So the kind of knowledge that we see in short supply is a more general kind, allied with overall insight and creativity, business judgment, and political wisdom.

Following glasnost, as the former Soviet Union has become increasingly open to information, its own natural *diversity* has also begun to flourish, in many cases uncontrollably. At first, the 16 republics asserted themselves, followed by the oblasts within the republics, and then even smaller units (cities and townships and many smaller ethnic groups).

Events lead us, at least in the case of the former Soviet Union, to the conclusion that the abundance of cheap information, together with freedom (which is apparently irrepressible if countries wish to be economically competitive), leads to the emergence of ever-increasing diversity. At the same time, however, genuine *knowledge* of how best to conduct our affairs in this unfolding process is by no means in surplus.

As obvious as this lack of knowledge is, however, the majority of people have a tendency to think of the process exactly backwards, as though the more information, freedom, and diversity we have, the more the world will automatically become unified. In business literature, the term *globalization* originally referred to the coming homogeneity of international markets. Today we understand that just the opposite is true. Global markets are becoming *more and more fractionated*.

In a free flow of information, as with a free flow of cheap energy, the main streets are lighted first, then the side streets, then the alleys, and finally the backyards and the smallest niches. The expansion of thought by a free population is like the expansion of such lighting.

In terms of business, what this means is that the main avenues for profit are explored first and the narrower opportunities

26

---------------- ✦ ----------------

Information, Matter, and Life

Each year, computers get smaller but more powerful. We read about a microchip that is ten times smaller and faster than the last one but that can compute ten times more.

The ability to compute, so it seems, is a fundamental property of matter itself. Individual molecules are apparently related to one another in a manner we used to call chemistry but which we now call "computation." The distinction between *information* and *matter* is all but gone.

The implication of molecules being information rather than "chemicals" is that the universe contains much more information than we previously thought—indeed, more than we could previously have *imagined*. There must also exist a much more complex set of patterns to the information in the universe than what was previously discerned. In this context, *life* itself can be seen as the most complex and interesting of all patterns of (molecular) information.

What life does is to organize information in such a way as to reverse the thermodynamic laws by which information behaves when life is not present. In other words, without life, patterns of information (matter) tend to become less and less well organized. This is the same as saying that without life things decay.

The amazing thing about life is that its very presence is a reversal of the decay and that living patterns of information (organisms), during their life, move from a state of less organization to a state of more organization. In lower forms of animals, this is called biological growth. In higher forms, the movement toward more organization is called the accumulation of knowledge or, in my terms, intellectual capital.

✧

The "Information Content" of Products

Consider two different companies that have the same sales volume in dollars. Company A has $100 million in sales and so does Company B. Company A manufactures hand-held televisions, with tiny two-inch screens. Company B, however, manufactures steel office furniture, such as executive desks and large file cabinets.

The shipping requirements of A and B are vastly different. Company A's $100 million of televisions can almost all be put aboard a single 747 aircraft. Company B's $100 million of office furniture requires several trainloads, or for export, a couple of ocean vessels.

What is gradually happening in the world is that there are many more companies like A than like B. Another way to say this is that the physical *weight* of world GNP is less and less, but its value is more and more.

Still another way to say this is that the *information content*, as opposed to the purely material content, of goods is going up. We are shipping more encoded information and less bulk.

One result of this trend is that world trade is easier and protectionism is harder. In the case of pure information, which is weightless, it is nearly impossible to stop a satellite from "shipping" messages across borders.

---

later. Niches and then tiny niches come last. Over time, markets do not become simpler and more unified, but much more diverse and complex. There are no longer a mere handful of brands in any market (of cars, cigarettes, toothpastes, or of any consumer good) but dozens and hundreds. The menu at a McDonald's restaurant does not get shorter, but longer and more diverse.

Likewise, in public life, congressional accord does not become easier with the passing of time but more difficult. Issues are not fewer but more numerous. Constituencies are not larger and more single-minded but smaller and more fractious. Lobbyists are not fewer in number but multiply with dozens of new points of view and interests to protect. Paperwork does not naturally become simplified, but ever more detailed and complex.

The fact that growth of information (the raw material) currently outpaces growth in general knowledge (the finished product) derives in large measure from the widespread misunderstanding of the linkage between cheap information, freedom, and diversity. Things naturally become more diverse, not less. The demand for general knowledge is enormous and accelerating, in part, because so much intellectual capacity is wasted in the attempt to formulate a single "Theory of Everything." The value of unified theories in a world that is becoming less unified, is, of course, limited. But despite the growth of information, freedom, and diversity, it is possible, as we shall discuss in this book, to greatly enhance one's stock of intellectual capital. The trick is to break away from today's most popular but erroneous "controlling ideas" and to adopt an unusual (but powerful) set of new attitudes.

4

Is Intellectual Capital in Business the Same Thing as "Brain Power"?

In the summer of 1991, the cover story of the June 3 issue of *Fortune* was called, "Brain Power: How Intellectual Capital Is Becoming America's Most Valuable Asset." The story was written by journalist Thomas A. Stewart.

I liked the title of this article right away. As an author of a book and a newsletter containing the term intellectual capital, I was naturally pleased to see the concept make the "front page" of the business world, and I want to review the article in detail here. What aspects of the concept did Stewart get right, and what aspects (if any) did he miss?

The "Brain Power" article is clearly written and is well worth reading. It is organized in six parts: (1) a definition of intellectual capital, (2) three case studies to show intellectual capital in action, (3) the two steps in finding and managing intellectual capital, (4) how the money markets measure and assign value to intellectual capital (if they really do), (5) how companies are presently trying to measure intellectual capital, and (6) the role of "networks" in increasing the flow of intellectual capital.

At various points in the narrative, Stewart makes some very good generalizations about intellectual capital. He says, for instance, "Harnessing your intellectual capital is not easy. It will force you to think hard about what kind of outfit you run, and maybe even change it significantly." This is certainly true. Furthermore, says Stewart, quoting partly from an executive at US West, "'Managing knowledge as an asset spawns whole new disciplines.' It alters how executives think about economics, technology, human resources, and planning." He is absolutely correct, and the idea of managing knowledge as an asset is highly desirable.

Finally, near the end of his piece, Stewart says, "Every company needs its own way to measure intellectual capital and the returns on it." This statement is also accurate, but its emphasis is wrong. It makes the whole concept sound as if it were a mere "detail of accounting." Instead, the real point of the article should be, "Every company has a unique kind and quantity of intellectual capital, which it must seek to understand, measure, and enhance over time." Unfortunately, the degree to which intellectual capital is singular, both for an individual and for a firm, is missed in the article, and the implication is wrongly made that something called intellectual capital can be easily measured and managed, if only the company has enough sense to listen up.

STEWART'S DEFINITION OF INTELLECTUAL CAPITAL

Stewart says, "Every company depends increasingly on knowledge—patents, processes, management skills, technologies, information about customers and suppliers, and old-fashioned experience. Added together, this knowledge is intellectual capital." In other words, "It is the sum of everything everybody in your company knows that gives you a competitive edge in the marketplace."

I agreed in general with Stewart, but I had two problems with his thesis. First, I wondered whether the word "sum" would be further clarified. I agree with Stewart that the intellectual capital of a firm is the sum of its individual parts, but the important question is how exactly is this kind of sum to be taken? How is addition to be performed on apples and oranges, or on elephants and ants? Will the ordinary rules of arithmetic apply? For instance, what if Albert Einstein works for the company? Will his portion of the total intellectual capital simply be "1 unit," or "1 PhD unit"?

Second, a principal component is left out of Stewart's definition; the missing element is the one on which practical enhancement of intellectual capital mainly depends. In my definition intellectual capital is the combination of (a) genetic inheritance, (b) education, (c) experience, and (d) attitudes about life and business. But nowhere in the *Fortune* article is attitude mentioned. Without this component, as we will see from the additional criticism that follows, the overall message of intellectual capital is *cybernetic*—an almost electromechanical vision of greater profits via controlling human beings as though they were intellectual automatons.

STEWART'S CASE STUDIES

After the basic definition, Stewart's article gives three examples of the presence of intellectual capital in American business. The first case involves the Polaroid Corporation, which had recently brought out a new medical imaging system in half the usual time, due (it says) to "interdisciplinary teamwork in the lab." The second involves Pioneer Hi-Bred International, where direct manipulation of DNA in petri dishes is saving years of time and thousands of acres of land formerly used for field testing, which is no longer necessary. The third case involves IDS Financial Services, a subsidiary of American Express Company, where computer software has been developed to codify the expertise of its best account managers for use by the entire rank and file.

The emphasis in these three examples is on the use of knowledge and technology to save resources (land, labor, and capital) and to increase the overall quality of services or products.

In considering the aforementioned cases, I can hardly object to the linkage of intellectual capital with what economists refer to as "relative efficiencies." The smarter a company is (i.e., the greater its stock of intellectual capital), the more likely that it can make things cheaply and well. But, at the same time, I have the feeling that in Stewart's view, the concept of intellectual capital and the idea of (merely) "technology" are coming out pretty much equal.

METHODS OF FINDING AND MANAGING INTELLECTUAL CAPITAL

After the three examples of what constitutes intellectual capital, Stewart turns to the question of how to get more of it. He says, "The first step in getting more from your intellectual assets is to find them." He cites a management consulting firm, Scientific Generics, that "helps companies map their technology assets— that is, locate them, define them, and lay out routes for getting them to other parts of the company."

This sounds very good, does it not? A logical series of steps: (a) locate, (b) define, and (c) lay out routes of transfer. If nothing more difficult than this is required, then a chapter called "Increasing the Flow of Intellectual Capital" can simply be added to college textbooks of electrical engineering.

At this point, I must confess to the onset of complete skepticism. As a management consultant, I am familiar with the power of promising that which ought to work, but which simply doesn't. The "technology mapping" scheme of Scientific Generics sounds a lot like something that really *ought* to work. Promises of this kind have eternal appeal because of a flaw in the executive mind that associates the degree of need with the power of logic: The more a business needs something, the more it believes in going about the pursuit of that something logically and the more it believes that this approach will work. In this case, if a business needs more intellectual capital, then it ought to be fruitful to pursue it in strict logical steps. This approach ought to work, but it doesn't.

"Step two" in augmenting a company's intellectual capital, according to Stewart, "is matching the company's intellectual needs with its strategic plan." The example here is once again Polaroid, whose management has made a systematic model of its hiring and training requirements for the future. Stewart goes on to say, "The forecast combines historical employee-turnover trends with data about the current work force, such as probable retirement dates, to estimate how many people with what skills will leave in the next decade. That information is then meshed with the company's long-range plan to show whether departing workers should be replaced by newcomers with similar or different training—a chemist by a chemist, or by a software engineer." On top of this, Polaroid "wants the present work force to equip itself for those jobs." "A worker who masters a skill that his department needs gets a raise, whether or not a promotion comes with it."

The idea of planning is good, but this example seems to be too elaborate and too top-heavy to succeed. The problem with an intricate "master plan" like this is in determining when management should deviate from it for the sake of unanticipated competitive advantages and, in the case of personnel, of unexpected "walk ons." Tough luck, if a young Einstein were to apply at Polaroid, unless of course he fit the intellectual capital plan, as stated: a set of college degrees, skills, and years of specific kinds of experience. People like Bill Gates or Stephen Jobs would not get in the door.

The idea of trying to pigeon-hole the kinds and quantities of human intelligence in order better to coordinate and manipulate them, is, of course, not new. But I am disappointed to see yet another attempt at this in the 1990s, linked as it is to what should be a much more powerful concept, namely intellectual capital.

"Once you've got a handle on your intellectual assets," continues Stewart—sounding for all the world as though any executive among us could actually accomplish this—"how do you package them? . . .The challenge is to capture, capitalize, and leverage this free-floating brainpower."

"One way is to automate it," says Stewart, before reporting a rather priceless quote from the CEO of a software design company in Pittsburgh. Dennis Yablonsky, of the Carnegie Group, says, "The time and energy invested in computers has gone into automating systems that relate to tangible assets—like payroll and inventory—not knowledge assets. Knowledge has been too hard to get to: It's in people's heads, it's *unstructured*" (italics added).

"No, Mr. Yablonsky!" I shouted as I read this quote. "I disagree. The knowledge is in people's heads all right, but it is *not* unstructured. In fact, you've got it exactly backwards. The knowledge in people's heads is in fact so highly structured that it cannot be programmed easily on computers."

A basic confusion in our culture has to do with the locus of genuine knowledge. We are taught as children that knowledge exists in books. But instead we learn from life that real knowledge exists in the minds of living people. The variety and strength of this knowledge is infinite. The structure of knowledge in each of us, whether or not we have the mind of Einstein, Gates, or Jobs, is singular. Our own knowledge is unlike that of any other human being.

The most important distinction made in this book is as follows: What exists in books is information. What exists in computers is information. What exists in the human mind is knowledge.

The confusion about information and knowledge, by the way, predates the appearance of computers. The literary critic,

———————— ✧ ————————

The Domain of Science

A friend of mine who is a successful lawyer once described to me his method of "preparing and controlling" witnesses. To my surprise, he compared this process to the way a truck driver concentrates on shifting gears along a difficult road. The role of the trial lawyer, in his view, was to drive the witness like a powerful machine through a complex terrain of evidence.

I ventured that while I thought he might be able to *rehearse* people before a trial and *coach* them through their performance, I doubted whether he could actually *control* them. A truck or any other machine can certainly be controlled but a person cannot.

The distinction between the domain of the humanities and the domain of science should be no more difficult than the comparison between a living person (in this case, a witness) and a machine (in this case, a truck). Science applies directly and powerfully to machines, but only haltingly and weakly to people. As individuals or as a species, we have as much capacity for emotion as we do for rationality; and as much as we might aspire toward greater logic in our lives and social affairs, it is the mix of head and heart that remains our essence.

The business intellect must function in both domains, humanities and science. Its greatest gains will be made the better it knows when it is crossing from one to the other.

———————————————————

T. S. Eliot, writing in the early 1940s, came to the same conclusion: "In our age, . . . men seem more than ever prone to confuse wisdom with knowledge, and knowledge with information, and to try to solve problems of life in terms of engineering."

HOW MONEY MARKETS MEASURE
INTELLECTUAL CAPITAL

In this section, Stewart observes correctly, "Seldom does a market ascribe value to intellectual assets." Part of the reason is our long tradition of accounting rules, which sees financial reality as directly associated with tangible assets. The Securities and Exchange Commission "holds that the fewer intangibles on the balance sheet, the better."

However, with the advent of "high technology," the markets' ideas of value can be seen to be changing. The stock market appears to be fully aware of the potential value of intellectual capital. If a ratio is taken, for instance, between the "book value" (or "physical replacement value") of a company and its "stock market value" (i.e., its stock price times the number of shares outstanding), this ratio will generally be much higher for companies like Microsoft than for companies like Emerson Electric. The ratio for Microsoft in 1990 was 8 to 1, for Emerson Electric, 2 to 1.

Many other factors than the "knowledge quotient," however, can affect stock market price, including downturns in the economy, new federal rulings on consumer safety issues or the environment, acquisitions and takeovers, and rumors of acquisitions and takeovers. It may well be that the money markets will display only a very rough capability to distinguish one company's (or industry's) stock of intellectual capital from another's.

HOW COMPANIES MEASURE
INTELLECTUAL CAPITAL

It is probably best to separate what the money markets measure—that is, earnings in terms of real money—and what companies measure, in an intermediate sense, to assist them in making more real money. In other words, it is best for the company to try to measure its own intellectual capital and to do so in ways that can lead to its enhancement and to its closer association with monetary results.

Here we come to a fairly recent but fairly well-accepted principle of modern competition that puts the concept of intellectual capital in terms of the company's "learning rate." Says Ray Strata, chairman of Analog Devices, quoted in the Stewart article, "The rate at which individuals and organizations learn may become the only sustainable competitive advantage."

Here is the frontier of our subject, the need of every company to find its own way of measuring its own intellectual capital. Stewart gives one very good example concerning on-time delivery—an intangible but nonetheless crucial element of gaining and holding customers and thus of earning better profits. "Analog Devices logged the monthly percentage of late shipments for each of its seven divisions for a year. One division cut the number in half every four months. Others were barely improving; that is, they weren't learning. By tying bonus plans to these results, the company awarded winners and motivated laggards."

The important suggestion here is to begin thinking about the key ways in which knowledge affects company profits and to begin measurement of the rate of learning in such areas, for despite our ability to define it well or not, intellectual capital is mainly of value when it is increasing, not when holding still and certainly not when decreasing.

The lesson in the Analog case, however, may or may not have to do with bonuses, per se, because the bonus structure of a firm may already be too complex to easily change. In this connection, the element of attitude arises, for in many cases the route to improved operations will not so much be money or complex computer programs but such things as "improved relations" between departments or of replacing haste in one part of a task with deliberate care and faithful records.

THE ROLE OF NETWORKS IN INCREASING THE FLOW OF INTELLECTUAL CAPITAL

The fascination with "networking" over the past decade, and in the Stewart article's last section, is based mainly on mathematical possibilities rather than what actually happens. The idea of a network involves the interconnectedness of many nodes, so that any single node can transmit to any other node and to the totality of all nodes (or some selected portion thereof) simultaneously. Thus, when a new node is added to a network, the total number of potential interconnections goes up as a power, not as a single number. If before there were 50 nodes in a network, all interconnected, then a single additional node adds not merely 1 but 50 new pathways for communications.

It seems to me without question that the use of computer networks for the entry, retrieval, and display of business records—whether of purchasing schedules, production levels, inventories, shipments, and customer order information—has made many businesses vastly more efficient. To say, however, that this by now "routine" use of computer networks has enhanced a company's stock of intellectual capital is a bit misleading. Equipment, after all, is not knowledge but merely equipment. Electronic records, in the same way, are also not knowledge but information. As I maintained earlier, the locus of real knowledge (and of what we are calling the intellectual capital of the firm) is in the minds of real people.

Whereas the automation of records has improved efficiency, I am dubious that the enormous expenditure of American business on "electronic mail"—the computer and software capacity to communicate among all the nodes on a company's network—can be said to have raised its overall intellectual capital. To make something available, even to mandate its use, does not guarantee the adoption of attitudes that will make the thing a success.

Human beings have perhaps more capacity to share among themselves than other earthly species, but humans also have plenty of fears and hangups that keep them from it, and a powerful desire to compete that "edits" every transmission. Human messages are never purely logical; they are often couched in the words of our common culture and are always, at least, half emotional.

Consider the popular concept of "interdisciplinary teamwork in the lab," cited by Polaroid in the *Fortune* article as the reason for the company's shorter development time for new products. I wonder how this teamwork was really achieved? Was it enough simply to have a "strategic hiring plan" that specified how many engineers, physicists, and chemists should be in a certain laboratory facility at a certain time? I found that we can be virtually certain that a great deal more "leadership talent" was involved because the mere juxtaposition of well-educated people who *should* mix does not in itself cause the mixing. Neither does it work to "command" such persons to mix for the good of company profits. The egos of persons capable of having original scientific ideas have basic needs of their own.

Many years ago, as a corporate research director, I oversaw a substantial new process investigation at an American university, in which the target was a better method for deriving high-quality food protein from oilseeds. I contracted with the university's research dean for time at the oilseed laboratory and I also contracted (with the dean's enthusiastic blessing) for support time with senior faculty in various of the university's other science departments, such as biology and electron microscopy. In addition, on my monthly visits, I regularly brought along other qualified scientists from other universities and from government laboratories working in kindred areas. "This ought to work very well," the dean and I both said.

But the lesson I learned was that I could not "push" the investigators into closer contact with each other, despite my control of the purse strings; competent scientists must want to do this of their own volition, or it simply does not happen. In my project, the competitive pressures between the various university departments and the outside laboratories were much greater than any kind of "joint knowledge appeal" that might be found for a genuine "interdisciplinary effort." The problem across university departments, or between universities, is possibly more difficult than within the R & D department of a single company. However, the corporate framework does not of itself completely remove the attitudinal forces that align themselves against the mixing of disciplines.

A person does not share a prime feature of his or her intellectual capital unless and until there is an environment of complete trust in the other people involved and in the disposition of whatever new intellectual capital (and monetary capital, but more so the intellectual capital) that might accumulate from the interaction. Furthermore, the disciplines involved in my project were all in the food sciences; the problem is an order of magnitude greater, for instance, if one tries to bring together more disparate fields, such as physics, chemistry, biology, ecology, and any of the humanities (like history, language, or philosophy). Often, when companies brag about a successful "interdisciplinary effort," they are speaking about bringing together experts from the sciences alone, such as an organic chemist, an inorganic chemist, and perhaps an electrical engineer.

THE BIG PAYOFF: INTELLECTUAL CAPITAL IN ECONOMIC OUTLOOK AND MANAGEMENT STRATEGY

What the *Fortune* article does is to introduce intellectual capital fairly well along a couple of its important dimensions in business, but not along several other directions that are of equal or greater importance. The article did a good job, for instance, of describing the relationship of intellectual capital to "operational efficiencies" and technology. The idea of using computer software to spread the expertise of the best workers to all the other workers is good; it should make the firm more efficient at what it presently does.

But how does the firm know when to change what it is presently doing? In other words, what is the role of intellectual capital in ascertaining the economic outlook that faces the firm? Furthermore, what is the role of intellectual capital in the setting of business strategy of the company versus its competition? Stewart describes rather glibly the process of "meshing" an intellectual capital hiring plan with the company's long-range plan. But what about the long-range plan itself? How many American companies have one? How many of these have a good one? Is this not the place for applying all the "brain power" (and more) that a firm can find?

Finally, going beyond planning to its intersection with reality, what part does intellectual capital play in meeting that supreme challenge in front of the CEO at all times, namely, to *integrate* the economic outlook and the competitive strategy? When is it time for a new plan? What "rules," if any, govern intellectual capital in these higher business functions, and how can the amount of intellectual capital available be enhanced?

5

Is Intellectual Capital the Same Thing as "the Intellectual Life" of Scholars?

ON THE WAY TO DES MOINES

I rarely read a newspaper article completely, from beginning to end. I did not make this a rule, it seems to happen on its own. In fact, I have often vowed to give more complete treatment to "important" stories (like the text of the President's State of the Union Address), but my resolutions always fail.

An exception occurred in the summer of 1992, however, while I was flying from Toledo to Des Moines, Iowa, in the case of a front-page story appearing in *The New York Times*. The story was not what typically appears on the front page, as it had to do with the arts and literature. It was a lengthy account of new research showing that, in the writing of *Huckleberry Finn*, Mark Twain had modeled Huck's colloquial speech pattern on a young black boy named Jimmy, whom he had met by chance in a big city, rather than on actual white speech in small-town

Hannibal, Missouri. A dozen or more comparisons between the speech of the young black boy (which Twain had detailed in a newspaper column predating the book by many years) and the speech of the hero of Twain's great American novel confirm that the way Huck speaks ("I was powerful hungry") owes everything to black dialect, not white.

The irony of this discovery is doubled by the fact that *Huckleberry Finn* is on the list of the "Ten Worst Offenders" in black studies today because it uses the word "nigger" over a hundred times and because it supposedly reinforces the status quo of white cultural domination. As we all know, however, it is one thing for a white person to use the word "nigger," and it is quite another thing for a black person to do so. But if the new research is correct, which one of these speakers is Huck, white or black?

So here indeed was a newspaper article I read from start to finish, enjoying every word. It seemed to me, as I deplaned in Des Moines, that the finding about Huck's black origins went a long way to justify the university resources devoted to literary scholarship (which I'm sure we all sometimes doubt) because it would shake up a lot of bureaucrats in education who thought that the case for teaching *Huckleberry Finn* or not was already an open and closed affair, or we might say here, a matter whose merits were "black and white."

With this instance of front-page multiculturalism as preamble, imagine my further surprise, as I headed north from Des Moines in a rental car, when I heard the local public radio station begin its daily half-hour "reading" program (devoted to the word-by-word narration of great books) with the announcer's saying, "We continue now with Chapter 37 of *Tom Sawyer*." I laughed aloud, "You've got to be kidding!"

The timing was perfect. I had 45 miles to go into "corn country," and by the time I got to my destination, Chapter 37 of *Tom Sawyer* had been fully read: Tom Sawyer and Becky Thatcher started out by getting hopelessly lost in a deep cave by the Mississippi River; but with good luck and fortitude, Tom finally found a new exit to the cave, five miles downriver from where they entered, and the day was saved.

Thirty years ago, as a graduate student of literature, I had read both *Tom* and *Huck* several times, but the long interval since college had made me forget the power of Twain's raw talent for telling a story. The episode in the cave, as the two kids burn their last candle and watch its final flicker, is scary.

Are Twain's novels not the kind of stories that any reader today will enjoy, whether white or black, male or female, oriental or occidental? Must we now have *Tom Sawyer* rewritten, so that Becky finds the way out instead of Tom? And in the rewrite, should we make Becky black, or perhaps "Native American" (Indian), or even Cajun? Can today's readers of literature make no allowance for the particularities and peculiarities of past culture? Is learning to do this not a central purpose in reading older works? Can the reader not forgive Twain, if need be, for his biases while still appreciating his art, or must today's readers instead be fed a stream of colorless generalities distinguished mainly by having been found to be "politically correct"?

ON THE WAY TO SIOUX CITY

These questions faded from my mind, of course, as my business day took hold, but as odd as it may seem, my "cultural encounters" with Iowa were not over with the *Huckleberry Finn* and *Tom Sawyer* episodes. About two weeks after my trip to Des Moines, I was once again headed from my home in Ohio to Iowa (by way of Minneapolis to Sioux City). In my reading materials for this trip was the Summer 1992 issue of *The Wilson Quarterly*, one of my favorite periodicals, which carried a long article called "The Cultural Wars; American Intellectual Life, 1965–1992," by Daniel Bell. I determined to break the rules again and read the article completely. "When headed to Iowa," I said to myself, "I must be destined to read something cultural."

I will not recapitulate what Daniel Bell (a scholar who appears on everyone's official list of "leading intellectuals") believes to have been the main outlines of America's intellectual life in the past three decades because, frankly, it makes for a very difficult and tedious read. Bell laments several times that "few individuals have come to the fore as intellectuals speaking to a wide public audience," but I'm afraid that he does little in his own writing to redress this situation. His style is what we all remember from school as academic, with intricate syntax, tough vocabulary, and (for me) obscure references. "No wonder I preferred Twain in college," I thought to myself in the middle of Bell's essay.

Actually, as I got into the essay, what sustained my interest the most was what Bell did *not* mention as being a part of "intellectual life," rather than what he did. For instance, in his list of public policy questions and intellectual concerns, he made absolutely no mention of the word *environmentalism*. My question is how could any "American intellectual" in the 1980s and 1990s not be interested in environmentalism, in the associated debate over natural resources, and in whether legislatively to restrict our consumption of fossil fuels—and thus (merely) to change the whole face of Western Civilization? On what grounds could Bell leave out an issue of this caliber, perhaps what might be one of the most critical driving issue of American politics in the 1990s, from his "American Intellectual Life, 1965–1992"?

Clearly, what Bell means by "intellectual life" and what I mean with my concept of intellectual capital are not the same. My special preoccupation with the intellectual demands of business apparently leaves me as far from the recognized center of "American intellectual life" as the fields of Iowa are from the prestigious universities on either coast of the country.

For Bell, the intellectual life is concerned with weaving a better and better net of such concepts as liberalism, conservatism, modernism, Marxism, capitalism, radical populism, family and religious idealism, poverty and inequality, political and moral philosophy, epistemology, law, economics, and literary theory, and most recently feminism, black studies, and multiculturalism. These concepts are important, and even crucial to the future of society and business, but I do not find them more stimulating now than they were as part of a required course in Western Civilization, and I do not look to "advances" in this quarter for genuine leaps in the organization of my intellect.[1]

MY LIBRARY IN TOLEDO

Of the dozens of books by the prominent intellectuals Bell mentions, only one was on my own bookshelf: *The Closing of the American Mind,* by Harold Bloom, which I purchased out of fascination when it rose to the top of the best seller lists several years ago, but which, after a few dozen pages, I was simply not able to read.

As I pondered the nature of the difference between the establishment intellectual and myself, a vision of the basic setup of my home library came to me and seemed illuminating. I have two large sets of bookshelves, one on either side of a fireplace. On one side, over the years, I have come to keep the "great books" from my days at the university—Shakespeare, Kipling, Frost, Hemingway, Yeats, Pound, Eliot, Orwell, Cummings, Sandburg, Connolly, Waugh, Wilson, Newman, Cassirer, Maritain, and other such names, plus a recent *Britannica.* I do not often read these books, but I cannot bring myself to toss them.

---

[1]Bell would surely say that the problem is mine not his. The "lack of interest" on my part is not his fault, and this same lack is everywhere seen in the American population. Even the leading journal for articles like Bell's (*Critical Inquiry*) has a circulation of only 3,700. But should we not ask whether this means that no one is interested, or that anyone with only general interest cannot penetrate the complexity of today's scholarly journals? Is it the burden of the listener to prepare adequately to hear the thinker, or of the thinker to find ways to reach the listener?

On the other side of the fireplace, more frequently used and more crammed with new titles waiting to be read, I have books such as the following (none of which are mentioned by Bell):

Julian Simon, *The Ultimate Resource* and *The Resourceful Earth*, each concerned with the enormous intellectual error involved in seeing the basic limit on man as his natural resources rather than his own imagination, understanding, courage, and wisdom.

Max Singer, *Passage to a Human World*, echoes Simon but with a penetrating chapter on what he calls "University Oriented Americans" (UOAs), who are so "well educated" that they cannot take ownership of a new line of thought without its being supported by some or another peer-approved study by a university and who, therefore, become the principal anchor for today's prevailing pessimism about man's future—inasmuch as what any official study does, by its inherent process, is to assign limits.

Michael Novak, *The Spirit of Democratic Capitalism*, concerns the role of human intelligence in any society but especially today's Western world. ("Creation left to itself is incomplete, and humans are called to be co-creators with God, bringing forth the potentialities the Creator has hidden. Creation is full of secrets waiting to be discovered, riddles which human intelligence is expected by the Creator to unlock. The world did not spring from the hand of God as wealthy as humans might make it.")

Freeman Dyson, *Infinite in All Directions*, concerns the role of humanity not just in society but in the universe at large, and the two poles of intellectual endeavor, *unity* (that is associated with the university) and *diversity* (that is associated with business). ("We have two main kinds of scientists, the unifiers looking inward and backward into the past, the diversifiers looking outward and forward into the future. Unifiers are people whose driving passion is to find general principles which will explain everything. They are happy if they can leave the universe looking a little simpler than they found it. Diversifiers are people whose passion is to explore details. They are in love with the heterogeneity of nature and they agree with the saying, 'Le bon Dieu aime les details.' They are happy if they leave the universe a little more complicated than they found it.")

Loren Barritz, *Backfire,* concerns the bureaucratic processes by which the United States became embroiled in the Viet Nam war, a central element of which was not so much intelligence or education, but *charm.* ("The higher one rises in a bureaucracy, the more important charm becomes, because the more important the bosses of the boss are, the more they are 'generalists,' the less they know, and the more they must rely on charm as an instrument of manipulation. Indeed, if one really goes high enough, the major questions of the board of directors, of the electorate itself, are questions of personality. Charm is the response to such questions.")

Paul Kennedy, *The Rise and Fall of the Great Powers,* concerns the thesis that all the great nations that have overextended themselves militarily have fallen—a concept he wants applied to the former Soviet Union and the United States, but one which I am dubious of and still debating.

Fernand Braudel, *Civilization and Capitalism; 15th to 18th Century* (three volumes) and *The Identity of France.* Let me hasten to insert here that Braudel is mentioned in the Daniel Bell article, but only in passing as a kind of mentor to another French historian of capitalism, Immanuel Wallerstein. In terms of both a scholarly and yet creative achievement, I know of no higher pinnacle than Braudel's, especially his third volume of *Civilization and Capitalism,* called "The Perspective of the World." Any intellect today who wants to know where capitalism came from, and upon what societal and terrestrial factors it most depended—and thus what its future may be—must read Braudel. At present, there is no shortcut to the long Braudel texts themselves, and the design of communication methods that could translate these master concepts to a broader audience deserves a high priority on the intellectual agenda of the 1990s.

Skepticism

If it is true, as I claim in this chapter, that America is a land of great abundance, then at least one item can be listed in short supply among its population, namely, the quality of simple skepticism.

By skepticism I mean the questioning of authority and public myth—not so much in our elected officials as in our culturally appointed high priests, our bank presidents, our professors, our doctors, our economists, our leading scientists, our nobel prize winners, our great intellectuals, and many others. It is not impolite for us to criticize our politicians, but the same is not true of our eminent scholars. To take on the likes of Daniel Bell, as I have done here, risks so much raising of eyebrows as to block acceptance by any "normal, American" reader.

But the kind of skepticism that I believe is healthy, and that I am certain builds greater intellectual capital for the business-person, is neither the complete irreverence of teenagedom nor the "philosophy of complete doubt" that first emerged in early Greece. Indeed, I have no real doubt about the possibility of greater and greater knowledge, just the opposite. The function of skepticism is to doubt *as a means to gain greater knowledge;* and the domain where this behavior regularly brings the greatest rewards is precisely when mere politeness is the barrier to greater insight.

ME VERSUS THEM

Another few dozen authors and titles could be cited here from the side of my personal library dealing with intellectual capital, as contrasted with the side dealing with the so-called intellectual life of Daniel Bell. But let me proceed to the three main points that come from this comparison of my approach with the establishment's. These points are made mainly in the sense of process, how we can use the work of other minds to enhance our own stock of intellectual capital.

First of all, my favorite books have to do with challenging the status quo in American thought, whereas the other books *are* the status quo, or at least a sample thereof, especially of the way it stood a few years back. I do not today choose what to read on the basis of studies, academic correctness, or peer review, but on what the gaps are in my present understanding of the world and on who seems to have the most powerful handle on filling in these holes. I confess to liking an author more if he or she shows himself or herself to be independent of approved thought in the university.

Second, the books that most enhance the growth of my intellectual capital are all written in plain language, despite their difficult and complex topics—in sharp contrast to *The Closing of the American Mind* (Bloom) or *Cultural Literacy* (Hirsch). Plain language is a tool of incalculable strength in guiding the mind to new and more powerful concepts and attitudes, enabling it in turn to add value to the universe in which it lives. The failure of academic intellectuals to emerge who can speak to us in simple speech, as noted by Bell, is sorrowful perhaps, but by no means fatal. The hungry mind knows to look elsewhere than the university today for food.

Third, if the omissions I have mentioned of authors, issues, and concepts from Bell's list were not by accident, then it is no wonder that he and I arrive at sharply differing assessments of present-day America, its future, and the role therein of human thought. In the concluding paragraphs of Bell's "American Intellectual Life, 1965–1992," he speaks of the loss of united vision, of cultural decay, of splintering, and of the troubling absence of any new unified beliefs to carry the country forward:

> The "project" that framed intellectual life during the past 200 years in the West has been utopianism and universalism, the direction of history laid down by the Enlightenment. Those larger visions have now receded and, in a different sense, the terrain in the West is now occupied by a cultural nihilism, a melioristic liberalism, and a conservative defense of traditional values, all of which are oriented to present issues. . . . We may be at the end of old ideologies and old History, but there are no unified sets of beliefs to take their place, only the splintering of cultures and political fragmentation. And this is the transition to the 21st century. (p. 107)

I have no doubt, of course, that America is much in need of repair and reinvigoration—if for no other thing, than its "intellectual life." But what Bell refers to as "cultural nihilism," insofar as I can understand this kind of label, is probably the exact sickness among academics mentioned by Max Singer: the habit of mind to rely on experts and studies for insight, rather than the direct assessment of the evidence oneself.

As to splintering and fragmentation, yes, we have it throughout. But as Freeman Dyson explains in *Infinite in All Directions,* the underlying tendency of the universe is to become more diverse, not less diverse. The world is not getting simpler with time, but more complex. This movement toward increasing complexity, however, has always been the case. Such a truth is alarming mainly to the mind that can see no future without central political (or cultural) control, that has no room in its beliefs for the thing Novak calls the spirit of democratic capitalism, and that is not driven (like the business intellect) to add value to the universe by an ever greater multiplication of its details.

And finally, with respect to a "unified overview," my own orientation is as follows: I wonder if the best way to see the problem with America is not more tied with its success than its failure and with surplus rather than shortage. In other words, why should it come as such a great surprise that the beliefs we have held for several centuries, aimed almost wholly at achieving material abundance, should need substantial revision when their mission has been so astonishingly achieved? And why indeed should we not now place such great emphasis on changing these attitudes?

6

Does Intellectual Capital Come Mainly from College Education?

REVIEW OF TERMS

In previous discussions of intellectual capital, I have listed its four main components (genetic inheritance, education, experience, and attitude) and I have spoken several times of the importance of attitude because I see it as the transmission fluid of the mix and the least difficult of the four elements to change. I have also mentioned the importance of balance between the four factors, and the fact that it is the excellence of the combination that contributes the most power.

Intellectual capital is singular in structure. It is different for each individual. It cannot be measured by a number on a unidimensional IQ scale. In particular, an IQ test does not address the element of attitude—of such human traits as curiosity, persistence, honesty, courage, resilience, irreverence (and thus creativity), and many others, all of which will be crucial determinants of whether our inherited abilities and education lead to productive experience. To add value to the world requires human beings who are hitting on all four of the cylinders I mentioned in defining intellectual capital.

As for the component of education itself, I have not previously singled it out—and so the impression I may have left thus far is that you should have it, that you should have lots of it, and that it should be largely "formal."

As we all know, however, not all education is equal and not all large "quantities" of education are necessarily good. Like anything else, education has a dimension of quality, and depending on this quality, along with the other elements in the mix, there is a right kind and amount of education that will genuinely enhance the structure of each person's intellectual capital, and bring it to a greater overall magnitude and power.

In this chapter, I want to take a more critical look at education, what makes it good (or not), and how it combines with the other three elements of intellectual capital.

The level of education I will be the most concerned with here is the college level, but this does not mean that I put less value on the "lower" levels, or even that I unquestionably recommend going to college. As a matter of fact, the question of college attendance today is becoming more deservedly uncertain. We read every day of the growing criticism of our university system, from within and from without, and we must seriously reconsider the advice we have given to our children automatically, which is at all costs to go to college.

WHO PROVIDES WHAT?

The first thing to understand about the concept of education, therefore, at least in my view, is that it is not something that is given but something that is attained. In other words, a willing student can obtain a good education in other ways than simply by going to college. The reading of good books, for instance, can take place elsewhere than on an ivied campus. The idea that an education can be packaged or "bottled," and then neatly dispensed to those customers with money, is a widespread American misconception. The associated idea that the seller of the package (e.g., a university) is responsible for its flawless delivery is likewise incorrect, as if education were a piece of software designed by Microsoft or Lotus, and installed by an accredited service center such as Ohio State or Michigan. Furthermore, the idea that a young person must attend college as a matter of discipline to "force" him or her to learn things is also an error—in which the element of attitude (i.e., willingness) is confused with the element of education. And finally, the view that a college education is essential as a "ticket" to better jobs, while not erroneous in the short term, emphasizes the goal of getting started on a career rather than the long-term goal of being able to add genuine value to the universe and to attain a kind and level of peace beyond the merely material.

Some readers will no doubt be slightly shocked by my list of irreverences, because the custom today (despite the intense criticism of our universities) is to revere and honor our academics, virtually beyond any other profession. The average American, upon being personally introduced at the same time to a university president and a senator, would not know to whom he should bow the most deeply. On this same scale of cultural esteem, a full professor might well outrank a city mayor or a leading banker or certainly a president of a corporation. I do not challenge the root of this respect, which has to do with the gratitude a student feels for a good teacher, but I think we might well be a little more critical of the myth of Academic Excellence—particularly when we are simultaneously wringing our hands over America's loss of competitiveness in the world economy and blaming it largely on our schools.

WHEN I WAS BUYING

The memories of my own time in college, and of later times when I took evening courses, are quite pleasurable. My formal education began in the mid-1950s and extended 25 years, to the late 1970s. It covered four major institutions and some 230 semester hours of courses of which 30 were in mathematics, 45 in physics, 30 in history, 45 in foreign languages and linguistics, 60 in English literature, and the rest miscellaneous. Whether or not I qualify as a legitimate critic of higher education is debatable but I must surely be ranked as a good customer!

Reflecting back on my purchases with present hindsight, the parts of my formal education that seem to me today to have been the most important are as follows: (1) the advisor (later the dean of liberal arts at Kansas) who allowed me to mix disciplines; (2) the same advisor again, who also allowed me to take senior-level "survey" courses (especially a course called "Survey of the Philosophy of History") as a sophomore; (3) a course called "The Introduction to Philosophy," covering Plato's Ideals and Aristotle's Four Causes, in which I got an "A-plus"; and (4) the mathematics courses altogether, not for the reason I then thought but because of the fact that having by now forgotten 90 percent of them, the sheer quantity I took in school means that what I do recall of mathematics today is relatively a lot, when compared to other businesspeople.

GLOBAL IDEAS

The principle that unites these items, in other words the thing that I most value about my formal education in later life, is the early practice with the integration of global concepts, together with ownership of the mix. I was allowed to choose the courses I wanted, purely on the basis of interest. Our intellect knows what kinds of pieces are missing from its own special puzzle, and it automatically seeks to fill in the gaps. An advisor who is steering a student toward a career rather than toward discovering the intellect's own agenda is reducing the student's long-term potential for adding value to the world (and ultimately for being as "happy" as he or she can be).

The globalness value is not so much true of Item 4, which I list mainly for its practical value in everyday business. But mathematics nonetheless has value in pulling ideas together, in quantifying the things that legitimately can be quantified, and in displaying the results clearly and powerfully.

The physics courses were also valuable, not only as a midlife confidence factor, as when today I encounter engineering matters in business, but also when I read scientific "baloney" on the policy front, as in the case of so much writing on global warming and other environmental issues. I remember vividly coming to the point in physics, in a course on nuclear physics, when I had to retrace the steps of Werner Heisenberg, proving to myself with full scientific logic that matter is as much a lightwave as a solid particle. I felt at the time that knowledge of the "Heisenberg Uncertainty Principle" would break me forever of relying purely on logic and of arguing for any single theory or any narrow point of view, no matter how well I might feel the evidence was set. (Such lessons, of course, have to be learned more than once!)

The languages I took as an undergraduate were entirely European; today I would give anything to have taken Japanese and/or Chinese, but in the 1950s neither I nor my advisors saw any great future for Asia. Equivalent errors are being made by students and professors today, even at the "greatest" of our universities, because regardless of how badly we may want to see the future, we cannot.

THE LOCUS OF KNOWLEDGE

Another misconception I had to work out of, and that is present more strongly in the university today, is the overall impression left on the college student that knowledge exists mainly in books and that people who have not read books or who cannot explain themselves well in academic language have no knowledge. As already mentioned, knowledge does not exist in books at all, but entirely in people. All people have knowledge, quite apart from whether they have had access to books. Many kinds of very important knowledge, such as business knowledge and political knowledge, cannot be learned from books but only from experience, that is, only from trying things directly in the market, failing, and then trying again. Businesspeople who have gained their knowledge in this fashion are often not able to speak in elaborate ways about what they know, how they know it, and how it can be passed on to junior associates. To insist that such businesspeople be able to explain themselves, as if part of a live Harvard case study, is to risk severe damage to their real knowledge, to their confidence, and to their individual stock of intellectual capital.

My prejudice about formal education, as is surely clear to the reader by now, is in favor of the humanities as opposed to applied sciences, and especially as opposed to several subjects that are called sciences but that are not—including political science, sociology, economics, education, and various others. I am not against knowledge of mathematics, physics, and chemistry, and I am not opposed either to engineering or technology. In my view, however, there is too much emphasis in today's university on how to run equipment (instead of on scientific inquiry itself) and too much faith that anything can be understood in terms of scientific logic. It will be of no surprise that engineering students today graduate with the conception that a colleague of theirs, let's say in economics, should be able to design an economy in much the same way as they design a building or a bridge—the big difference being simply in substituting econometrics software for CAD-CAM software.

IS KNOWLEDGE ANOTHER FINITE (LIMITED) RESOURCE?

Another interesting issue among educators today, and also among certain businesspeople, is the concept that the United

States will soon "run out of scientists and engineers," probably before the end of this century. The view is based on an extrapolation of the enrollment levels of the late 1980s and projected corporate openings, which show a big gap developing in the late 1990s. In this popular supply-demand model, however, the key factor of *price* is always omitted—which, of course, suits businesspeople, for they are loathe to advocate paying a higher wage and they see nothing wrong with going along with the educators' view that some fixed percentage of kids ought to become scientists willy-nilly, almost as if by patriotic duty. As the price for scientists and engineers rises, however, the gap will be filled either by Americans or by "imports." The educators and businesspeople who leave price out of the analysis also leave out imports, as though we must all agree that American science and engineering jobs, for the good of the country, must ultimately be filled with Americans, by which they generally mean White Anglo-Saxons, and not even Recent Asian Americans.

Another aspect of this misconception of science education is that it should be the role of the university (or of secondary schools earlier on) to explain science in such an enjoyable way that the instruction motivates students to continue on, eventually toward their PhDs. This particular error rests on two other misconceptions: (1) that science is inherently easy to understand (it's not, it's *hard*), and (2) that motivation is furnished to a student from without (it's not, motivation must come from *within*). As time passes, the world becomes ever more complex, not simpler. Science and technology are becoming more diverse every day at a startling rate. There is no "grand unified theory" from which to start or that can be swiftly taught to students, as by a tutorial masterstroke. There are principles, yes, even simple principles, but the distance from simple principles to the complex frontier of new applications has become a tedious set of long, branching pathways between hundreds and thousands of microspecialties. It should be no great surprise that this is a difficult network of knowledge to learn, or that students should feel that the rewards (the pay) should be high.

ANOTHER PROBLEM FOR THE EXPERTS?

Compounding all errors upon errors is the most fundamental error of all and that is the idea that more science is what we need, as opposed to more intellectual capital, defined in the broad sense with which I started this book. Finally, delaying the call for amateur diagnoses such as the one above, comes a final paradox: our cultural insistence upon the use of recognized experts to fix anything of great importance, which means that the problems with college education are handed back to the college educators themselves, the ones with the most credentials from inside the system they must try to fix. Judging by how long it has taken for American business to learn to listen to its customers, we may have a long while to wait for academic experts to learn the same thing.

7

Is Intellectual Capital Organized in Completely Logical Fashion?

The fascinating thing about the news in America is the speed with which a new topic can gain predominance and the disparity between issues that get the same sized headlines. Neil Postman calls this "a peek-a-boo world, where now this event, now that, pops into view for a moment, then vanishes again."

In the fall of 1991, for instance, and without any warning, Magic Johnson's infection with HIV took over the front page of public consciousness, despite the fact that we should probably have been paying much greater attention to the unraveling of Soviet communism, to the possibility of North Korea's having an atomic bomb, or to our own inability to snap out of an economic recession.[1] The Magic Johnson case was not "more important" than all these other issues of world affairs, it was simply important in an entirely different way. How exactly did he get the

[1]The fact that in early November 1991, British scientists achieved a two-second-long, two-megawatt burst of electricity from a pure fusion reactor, the culmination of a 50-year quest since nuclear energy was first discovered, is a mere footnote carried in *The New York Times* but nowhere else.

virus, what would it be like to be a multimillion dollar sports hero with all the "pleasures" of life available, and what would happen now? How long would he live? Would he really go ahead and play in the Olympics? (Yes.) When will we have a cure? Will AIDS prove forever incurable, a kind of moral plague spreading to all sectors of society, regardless of our sexual proclivities?

In each and every 52-week period, this process of one story's being trumped by another takes place dozens of times. We can scarcely remember what was on the front page a year or more ago. The Persian Gulf War of 1990–1991, for instance, is a faint recollection. The Soviet Coup of August 1991 has come and gone. The Clarence Thomas hearings are over. The Gates hearings are over. (Was he appointed as CIA Director or as Attorney General?) The Kuwait oil fires are out. (Weren't they going to burn forever?) Cease-fires in the Yugoslavian civil war have come and gone. Peace talks between the Arabs and Israelis have commenced, but when and where will they continue? The "message" of the 1990 *off-year* elections has come and gone. (What was the "message" again?) The Secretary of State took time off from the Mideast to go to China, but he came home with no concessions on trade. (Will Congress impose new sanctions against China? Or will Congress be too busy with another scandal or another hearing? Will Congress ever finish with the Iran-Contra affair?)

President Bush, who at the moment of victory in the Persian Gulf War in 1991 seemed politically invincible, 52 weeks later became fully vulnerable because of his seeming failure to possess or to communicate something everyone is calling a "domestic vision."

No sooner do we have a grasp of the "big picture" than it changes and moves beyond our focus. No sooner do we get the pieces arranged than the symmetry is broken. Almost every day a new card is dealt, which changes the entire hand and the whole game. As much as we would appreciate more time to study each fresh configuration, the pace of the dealer continues to quicken.

The cards in a Bicycle playing deck, even after extensive shuffling, are perhaps more logically interrelated than the cards of the daily news. At least, the playing cards have predesignated numbers and suits (ranks), whereas the cards of the daily news are all potential new trumps and jokers, whose eventual magnitude is unknown when first dealt. The business of journalism is to add a more and more sensational trump card every day.

On top of this, of course, to extend my analogy a little further, the name of the "real" game and its rules are only vaguely known and agreed to by all the players. Getting ahead, especially in politics, often involves relabeling the game (e.g., "The New Deal," "The Fair Deal," etc.) and changing the rules.

Americans whose entire mental life has been spent at the media table, watching a thousand new trump cards unfold, are sometimes said by Europeans not to have a world view. (No *weltanschauung*, a German scholar might say.) What this criticism means is that as a people we do not display a powerful grasp of history or of long-term economic principles.

Many critics have zeroed in on television as the culprit. Let me quote further from Neil Postman in *Amusing Ourselves to Death*. The "peek-a-boo world," he says, "is a world without much coherence or sense; a world that does not ask us, indeed, does not permit us to do anything; a world that is, like the child's game of peek-a-boo, entirely self-contained. But like peek-a-boo, it is endlessly entertaining." Furthermore, "embedded in the surrealistic frame of a television news show is a theory of anti-communication, featuring a type of discourse that abandons logic, reason, sequence and rules of contradiction. . . . A person who has seen one million television commercials might well believe that all political problems have fast solutions through simple measures—or ought to. Or that complex language is not to be trusted, and that all problems lend themselves to theatrical expression. Or that argument is in bad taste, and leads only to an intolerable uncertainty." Television is "a medium which presents information in a form that renders it simplistic, nonsubstantive, nonhistorical and noncontextual; that is to say,

--- ✧ ---

Hypercard

The ultimate in electronic card games, for those readers familiar with the Macintosh computer, is Hypercard.[1] A Hypercard stack is like a real stack of 3 by 5 cards, except that in the computer version, the cards can all be linked by "buttons" and "menus." The cards all begin life with equal weight, until and unless the author of the stack assigns them and their information content some special value, or some special address. This is the same way we treat the profusion of cards from journalists: We ignore the headlines and treat the stories with whatever rank we feel appropriate.

The drawback to electronic stacks, if indeed it ultimately proves to be one, is that we can only see a single card at a time. In other words, we do not regularly put two cards side by side and compare them for their logical consistency. Instead, each card tends to fill our consciousness separately. One card may proclaim, for instance, the high quality of an Acura automobile and another card later in the stack may decry the American trade deficit; the fact of our desire for high-quality products is automatically separated in the stack from our concern for the future of our own work force. The net effect of larger and more rapidly moving "information stacks" is to increase our intellectual tolerance of logical contradiction.

[1]In the DOS/Windows world, an equivalent software program is called "Toolbook."

---

information packaged as entertainment. In America, we are never denied the opportunity to amuse ourselves." Postman would like to see the country return to a greater "print orientation" that replaces "peek-a-boo," "trivial pursuit," and amusement with a genuine invitation to think and to reflect. But the reality is otherwise, for as he concludes, "Americans will not shut down any part of their technological apparatus, and to suggest that they do so is to make no suggestion at all. It is almost equally unrealistic to expect that nontrivial modifications in the availability of media will ever be made."

At the risk of seeming unpatriotic in the face of Postman's concern for our country, let me hasten to say that my purpose in presenting his view so thoroughly is not to urge widespread social reform of electronic media. Rather, my goal is to establish, as realistically as possible, the setting for increases in intellectual capital which, as I have emphasized already, is a decidedly singular and *individual* phenomenon. No intellect in America today can simply turn away from television, from the incessant 52-week peek-a-boo of the news, and still expect to be in full touch with the economy, politics, and business of the country. The job of the intellect, in this case, is not so much to advocate general change as it is to make its own particularized changes: to simultaneously stay in touch while perhaps "pulling back" to make even greater touch by means, for instance, of a more powerful program of "competitive reading" and other techniques covered in other chapters of this book.

It may be, too, that our American way of flipping through cards and lightly browsing through a deluge of information is ultimately more powerful than the old methods of carefully constructed patterns of cause and effect. Certainly, we should not expect the diversification and multiplicity of daily events to cease, nor the intensity of journalistic competition and sensationalization to ease. Why try to be completely logical about a process that is inherently chaotic?

Whichever way of adapting turns out best, however, "intellectual hypercard" or "focused *weltanschauung*," today's politicians must live and die by the flipping of cards in the public consciousness. The demand for the president to have a "domestic vision" (which means some kind of broad, well-structured, long-term plan) is obsolete. Our social attention span is too short to execute such programs. The whole issue will be trumped a dozen times between now and the next 52 weeks.

8

Why Is Attitude the "Transmission Fluid" of Intellectual Capital?

Of the four elements that combine to produce intellectual capital (genetic inheritance, education, experience, and attitude), attitude is the easiest one to change, especially in later life. Although I am sure of this point, it is not *easy* to change. In fact, changing a person's attitude toward even a seeming trifle—whether he or she salts food, whether he or she prefers Coke or Pepsi, or whether he or she reads *The Wall Street Journal* or *The New York Times*—is extremely difficult.

Often, a person's attitudes are changed only by the "rude awakenings" and major traumas of life. Sometimes, however, an attitude can change almost immediately when triggered by a new insight, a new way to see an old problem, or a completely fresh set of ideas. This book, of course, seeks to open the latter route rather than the former, and the rest of these pages are devoted to an eclectic mix of insights, suggestions, and exercises that have produced attitude changes (occasionally and unpredictably) for the author and others.

In calling attitude the "transmission fluid" of the mix, my intention is to convey directly the ultimate *power* attitude has in expanding our knowledge. But a conscious and willful desire to produce a change in attitude does not often work; therefore, I want to refer to attitude in more indirect ways than as an auto-motive fluid. Although the parallelism is not complete, this more delicate approach brings to mind a process in poetry called *synaesthesia*.

In a favorite poem of mine by Emily Dickinson, written about 120 years ago, the first two verses go as follows:

"There's a certain Slant of light,
Winter Afternoons—
That oppresses, like the Heft
Of Cathedral Tunes—

Heavenly Hurt, it gives us—
We can find no scar,
But internal difference,
Where the Meanings, are—"

These lines have always worked well for me in combining multiple images. The poet first calls light a sound, then gives sound a weight, and then mixes all three senses with *meaning*. It is, I think, synaesthesia at its very best.[2]

Let me now embark on broadening and mixing the idea of attitude in the formation of intellectual capital; I want to link it with the *software* side of the "hardware-software" metaphor for the duality of body and mind.

---

[2]The striking thing about the appearance, today, of poetry in a book of prose is the reduction in reading speed it commands of the reader. Unless you are willing to "gear down" and let the verse work at its more modest rate, you will miss the intended effect altogether. Our busy lives carry over to our reading. We are so intent on maintaining a rapid scan that the presence of poetry is often found more annoying than relaxing. This is another clear sign that our *attitude* needs changing. If a poem (or a picture in an art gallery) brings us a genuinely fresh and useful idea, what difference does it make that we must change our gait? Indeed, why would we ever suppose that a *steady* gait, fast or slow, would be the most intellectually productive? Should we not accept the guidance of common sense, that a "change of pace" is good for the soul (and for the development of intellectual capital)?

Let us first observe that our body has been with us for a very long time, pretty much as we see it today, with feet, legs, trunk, heart, the other organs, and our head. Then let us ask, "But what of our mind, has it been the same all along?" Consider Figure 8-1, which gives an estimate of human life expectancy over the last five thousand years, a period encompassing virtually all of what we speak of as "civilization." In 3,000 B.C., according to archeologists, the average life span of a human being was 18 years; during Roman times, 26 years; during the Middle Ages and into Pax Britannia, 35 to 45 years; and just a hundred years ago, as the twentieth century was about to begin, about 50 years. Today, in the early 1990s, our life span is about 76 years, and is headed up toward 85 years by the end of the century.

We are generally aware of the changes in sanitary conditions, nutrition, and medicine that have made these recent increases possible. However, my position is not so much concerned with the progress itself as with the hardware-software issue. If the body is the "hardware," and if this hardware was in some sense "designed" for a service life of some 85 years, then is it not remarkable to find that it took so many centuries to push the design limits of the "hardware"? And if the mind is the "software" in this two-part structure, then why should it be a surprise that much of the burden of the change, in going from a life span of 18 years to 85 years, has been carried by the mind? Is it any wonder, therefore, that history has seen so many "software programs" go by in myth, song and rhyme, poetry, reason, enlightened reason, scientific thought, mercantilism, capitalism, industrial capitalism, democratic capitalism, Marxism, Communism, and dozens of others?

An interesting thesis in this connection about the "duality" of mind-body was put forward by Julian Jaynes in his 1976 book, *The Origin of Consciousness and the Breakdown of the Bicameral Mind.* In Jaynes's view, the emergence of language and culture over several thousand years of civilization had the effect of virtually "rewiring" the two (formerly independent) hemispheres of the human brain, and, thus, giving rise to "conscious-

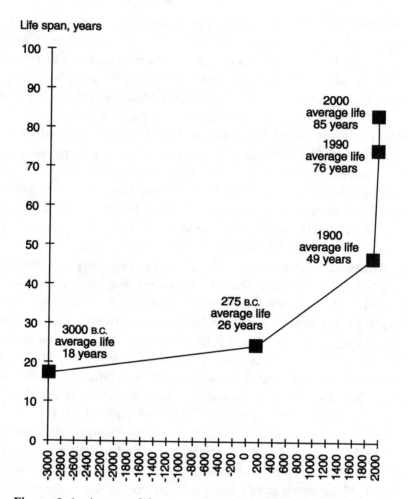

Figure 8–1 Average life expectancy since the bronze age. (Data from Peter Gorner and Ronald Kotulak, "Do We Want to Cure 'Aging'?" *The New York Times*, December 15, 1991.)

ness." We are conscious through the faculty of language, Jaynes says, and in the ability of one cerebral hemisphere to "listen" to the other. Whether or not this is true, this viewpoint helps us to appreciate the past power of our "software" and the enormous potential that remains from this side of the equation, for it would be hard to expect as much gain from the old "hardware" itself, the body and its organs. In other words, if there is to be a potential for greater knowledge, it must come from the software side (controlled by what I call our *attitudes*), not so much from the hardware.

The key to my approach for making changes in attitude requires unbundling the concept from the larger idea of culture and "cultural attitudes." My goal is not to change our culture, my goal is to open the door to individual change among a small number of interested readers, and it is hoped that it will be a worthwhile contingent. In fact, for such individuals to change, no change at all is required in the culture: *We already have complete freedom of choice among any attitudes we can possibly name.*

The kind of thought that results from the changes I recommend is known as "independent thought." It is the opposite of the kind of thought that Max Singer, in his book *Passage to a Human World*, identifies with "University Oriented Americans" (UOAs):

> The kind of person I have in mind as a member of Category UOA is one who directly or indirectly looks to the academic world as the highest source of truth and wisdom. . . . UOAs are the kind of people who, in case of doubt, believe arguments and facts that seem to come with the right intellectual credentials (whether the *Journal of Sociology, Time* or the senior TV pundit). . . . Members of Category UOA look to recognized academic experts and to university leaders as the most admirable people, those whose views are most to be respected, whose values and styles are the highest standards. . . . In general, university-oriented people regard information that comes from books, or media reports of "studies," as the best information or the only serious and reliable information. Personal experience, the views of ordinary men (who haven't done or read a "study"), and common sense or simple analysis, are all seen as second class sources of understanding. (pp. 232–233)

The kind of person who is *not* a member of Singer's UOAs and the kind of person this book is aimed at helping are people

Figure 8–2 The single human intellect and the world of information. Independent thought requires direct access to evidence, deliberate selection from surplus, and full ownership of interpretation.

who "could be UOAs but whose *attitude* is different" (italics added). Such people are well and highly educated. They "do not deny the intellectual power of scholarship and science, but it is not what they value most highly. They are used to trusting their own judgment. They care more about effectiveness than style or

A Good Lecture

In much the same way that a poem or a picture can "break the pace" of modern intellectual life, so too can a good spoken lecture.

Unlike newspaper and television journalism, a lecture does not need to be couched at the eighth-grade level. Furthermore, conclusions can be built up gradually and supported all along with detailed evidence, instead of being featured as opening salvos in a contest to outsensationalize other reporters and other stories. Another way to say this is that following the daily news is not intellectually challenging in the way that sound academic thought can be, when it is well-organized, rigorously documented, and clearly phrased.

The challenge of a good lecture can be threatening to a businessperson who is used to a constant diet of lighter material. The fear comes from the potential of having to give up comfortable but ultimately insecure positions in one's world view—positions introduced by journalism but never fully tested or fortified.

other credentials, and their normal recourse is to experience and wisdom rather than the ideas that have filtered out from academia. They live by their understanding that the scholarly community has not yet achieved its ideal of self-correcting behavior, and of humility before the complexities and uncertainties of the world."

With the goal of such independent thought in mind, let us now proceed to Parts Two and Three of this book. Part Two is designed to challenge the role of authority in our intellectual life, and Part Three is designed to enumerate simple exercises in building more productive intellectual attitudes.

PART TWO

◇

Breaking with Authority

9

Tackling Big Institutions

The Case of the World Bank and the CIA

THE WIDESPREAD BELIEF IN EXPERTS

Throughout the year, the media tell us of the release of important reports by such major institutions as the United Nations, the World Bank, the International Monetary Fund, departments of the U.S. federal government, major universities, and hundreds of panels formed from eminent authorities. "UN Adds a Human Element," said a 1990 headline about a planning document released by the UN Development Program. "Commodity Failure Central to African Crisis," said another headline about a report by the UN's Trade and Development Task Force. "Report by World Bank Sees Poverty Lessening By 2000 Except in Africa," said another. "Record Transfer of Resources to Industrialized World, Says Bank," "U.N. Sees a Crisis in Overpopulation," and "A Greener Bank: The World Bank's new World Development Report argues that wise environmental policies may often make poor countries less poor." When authorities disagree, even larger headlines always follow: "UN Report Challenges World Bank Africa Study."

Much of the overflow of information generated today is in the form of books and reports by multiple authors, teams of people who are each experts in narrow disciplines. What the reader must remember is that the tossing together in one bowl

—————————— ✧ ——————————

Absolutes

In Plato's *Phaedo*, which dates from about 400 B.C., Socrates asks Simmias:

> "Do we say that there is such a thing as absolute justice, or not?
> Indeed we do.
> And absolute beauty, and absolute good?
> Of course.
> Have you ever seen any of them with your eyes?
> Indeed I have not, he replied."

With respect to the power of absolute ideas over the intellect, I often wonder how much progress has been made in the 2,400 years since Socrates' questions. In addition to the ideal concepts of justice, beauty, and good, we have hundreds of others today, which range from truth in advertising, decisions based on science (not emotion), and equal employment opportunity, to scholarly studies, experts, megatrends, new world orders, ecological balance, and sustainable growth.

Who of us has seen any of these with our own eyes? Who has seen, for instance, an *expert* whose *forecast* of the *economy* turns out to be correct? And yet, who does not anxiously await the next such prediction? Do we not demand pledges from politicians? Do we not all desire progress, a balanced budget, and World Peace?

If the mind were not organized around the eternal possibility of its ideals, how would we sustain hope for the future? But at the same time, for the intellect seeking superior knowledge, what more immediate route is available than breaking the control of its own ideals?

of their various writings, even when these conform to a designated outline, does not result in a coherent world view. The parts of such a report are mixed superficially but are still essentially separate. The parts do not fuse into an assembly with an inherently higher order of intellectual value. These higher assemblies are produced by the single human mind. A powerful world view will certainly *depend* on the inputs of many experts, but it will be drawn together and raised in value only by the individual.

A widespread error today, which must be recognized by those seeking better world views themselves, is to revere the compilations of teams of experts as if the product represented a powerful world view when in fact it does not. We must reject the view that a report by a panel of experts is better than a report by a single person, especially since the individual may have sterling credentials, be very forceful in the art and science of integrating, and have the ability to pull things together.

An even more dangerous extension of this mistake is to believe that the existence of, say, *The Handbook of Chemistry* implies the existence, somewhere, of a master chemist who knows and understands all of what the handbook contains. Or that the existence, say, of a "world report" implies the existence of a world expert who understands the world.

Accepting the myth of world experts prevents the individual from believing that his or her own world view can have great potential power, and from taking steps to enhance it. There is today a kind of unspoken assumption that trusting one's own view is arrogant and that to be socially proper we must defer to those who really know the subject. In so doing, of course, we must assume that such people really exist.

The widespread belief in experts inhibits the teaching of what we mean by "world view" especially at the elementary level, where it would have the greatest positive effect. The original German word for the concept, *weltanschauung*, is taught only at graduate levels of literature and philosophy, and rarely if ever makes its way into the teaching of business. And yet, in sharp irony, American businesspeople are continually accused of "not understanding the world" as well as the Japanese, the Germans, and many others. The problem is that their culture first tells American students that they are not supposed to understand things as well as "professionals" and that *someone else* will do it for them. It is impolite to see yourself knowing as much as *the experts.* It is impolite to disagree, for instance, with the Federal Reserve about monetary policy, with the International Monetary Fund about balance of payments, with the United Nations about food and population, or with the World Bank about poverty and development. It is perhaps most impolite to disagree with a panel of distinguished scientists who have concurred together in a report that the world is entering global warming.

To have your own independent views of important matters will be seen by many people as amateurish. In terms of our own business success and careers, however, it is the "amateur championship" that matters, not the professional.

Weltanschauung

The German word *weltanschauung* means "world outlook" or "world view." In this country, the word has been used mainly in literary criticism, referring to the prevailing spirit and vision of a period, as encapsulated in the works of a particular "great writer"—for instance, Thomas Hardy's view of the human being as a victim of fate and circumstances.

The idea that each of us does and should have a world view—that we should claim ownership of it, that it should be critically examined and enlarged, and that it is a key platform from which to expand intellectual capital, is a recent novelty.

———————— ✧ ————————

Experts

An expert in major league baseball can make many millions of dollars a year by hitting safely about 30 percent of the time. On rare occasions, certain superstars average 40 percent. An expert professional basketball player, to earn a similar fortune, must sink 60 percent of his field goals, and more than 70 percent of his free throws.

Outside the domain of sports, however, experts can be experts without such numerical track records. Oddly enough, no one keeps averages on the forecasts of famous economists, futurists, and visionaries. No one checks on the outcome of recommendations by big name business consultants. And no one doubts that an expert tax lawyer knows how to save him or her money, 100 percent of the time.

Would the habit of keeping track change our minds about what an expert really is? Consider, for instance, the Internal Revenue Service. Audits of the IRS's own tax advisers show that their advice to taxpayers is correct 70 percent of the time. (Yes!) Which of us, however, has the courage to apply these odds to our own return? Which of us indeed has enough confidence even to argue (silently) with famous authorities, let alone to dismiss them out of hand?

WHAT IS THE WORLD VIEW OF THE WORLD BANK?

To probe these notions further, let us consider a specific example of a multiple-author report. During the past decade, the World Bank in Washington, D.C., began issuing an annual publication called, "World Development Report." Typical of the series, the 1988 report was 307 pages long, over half an inch thick, printed on top-quality 8 by 10 1/2 paper, and in full color. The report contained 10 chapters, 73 figures with text, 55 special "boxes" of text and figures (case studies and examples), 33 statistical tables (covering 67 pages), 17 pages of technical notes on how the statistical tables were compiled, 3 pages of definitions, acronyms, and initials, and one 10 by 16 erratum table apologizing for an error in exchange rates in one of the appendix tables.

A word count of the report indicates that a dedicated reader, proceeding at 250 words per minute, could finish the book in three days, given no interruptions. However, the character of the report suggests that few if any such readers actually made the effort.

You may ask, "What? No one in the world has read the 'World Development Report 1988'?"

My answer is no. A few senior economists may have read *in* it, but none of these will have read it completely. A few senior policy makers and their staff will have read *some* of the ten-page *overview*, but I sincerely doubt that any of these finished the overview itself or went any further in the report other than to scan it. A large number of professors received the report gratis from the Bank, flipped through the pages, and put it on one of their thick piles of material "to be read." A few business researchers probably browsed through the book, admired the three-dimensional, four-color graphs, and started to read some of the boxed case studies; but I doubt that any of these researchers spent more than half an hour in total examining the book. As many as a dozen journalists, perhaps, filed stories on the report's conclusions when it was first published, but they worked from the press release version of the overview.

The lack of readership certainly does not square with the importance of the book's topic. Nothing could be more vital than the theme of the "World Development Report 1988," namely, the relief of poverty in developing countries by means of wise public policy and the judicious enabling of private enterprise. But we can be virtually certain that no one in the world, excluding the author, actually read the report.

And what about the author? The report was not exactly "authored" but "prepared," it says in the front, by a team of 15 people, led by a certain Johannes F. Linn, and assisted by support staffs of statisticians, editors, computer artists, and other production workers. Mr. Linn himself, as team leader, surely did not write the entire text or the majority of it, nor did he even "outline the entire outline." My guess would be that his toughest job was negotiating the manuscript through a tortuous approval channel within the Bank, during which literally hundreds of other experts had a crack at the team's conclusions and prose. Mr. Linn probably saw himself as the report's "coordinator" or "assembler," receiving raw materials from many different people and uniting these materials in one format. Providing consistent grammar, adding color graphics, and printing the text in a matched set of fonts is only superficial unification—that of the printer's, not of the intellect's. The content was not digested, nor could it be, by a single human mind and then reassembled at a higher level.

So the author of the report is not what we usually mean by an author, that is, the mind of a single person. The author is really the World Bank, the bureaucratic institution itself. The audience of a report so authored is not individuals but other institutions, by which we mean the teams of experts in such other institutions that will have read *in* the book, much in the same way as those in the Bank's own approval channel did, looking for objectionable particulars and flaws in the narrow domains about which they have detailed knowledge.

The "World Development Report 1988" is, in other words, a *handbook* of information about the world of the World Bank, its policies and problems, and not a coherent essay about how to fix things and not a "book" that the intelligent lay reader can "grasp," the way we conventionally mean those words. Handbooks provide information but not knowledge.

At the risk of pushing the present reader beyond the edge with this one example, let me continue. The case study boxes in the "World Development Report," which make up half the text, cover topics such as "Recycling Japan's funds" and "Measuring the public deficit," along with "Food subsidies in Mexico,"

"Performance of public bus companies in two Indian cities," "Divestiture of state-owned textile mills in Togo," "Implementing educational reform in Ghana," and "How do Nigerian manufacturers cope with inadequate infrastructure services?" These and the other 50 special boxes in the report are in effect summaries of separate "PhD dissertations." Each underlying dissertation is a compilation of findings by hundreds of World Bank teams working in all of the world's countries. Each team is made up of specialists in finance, taxation, transportation, textiles, food, education, and dozens of other disciplines.

Upon investigation by a team of experts, any one small subject, however limited it may at first seem, for example, a public bus company in Calcutta, expands into a vast universe of complexity. To summarize the immense findings (the "dissertations") on two such subjects into a bare 400 words in a single box in an annual report will seem like gross oversimplification to the original compilers of the information. Thus, if you ask a representative of the World Bank about the quality and depth of "World Development Report 1988," he or she will likely say that it only scratches the surface, that it does not give the full or true picture, and that it oversimplifies things dangerously.

HOW INTELLIGENT IS THE CENTRAL INTELLIGENCE AGENCY?

Archimedes, the Greek inventor of levers, said, "Give me a solid place on which to stand, and I will move the world." The problem with Archimedes' request is that there are no really solid places—a fact that is just as true now as then, and is true for concepts as well as engineering work.

Consider the decline of communism, the sudden collapse of the Iron Curtain, and then the reunification of Germany, all of which took place in the short period between 1989 to 1990. Before these events happened, I wonder how many Americans believed, as I did, in communism's permanence? It was a single concept that would never die, a principle around which all of our other foreign affairs could be oriented. Communism was bound to last forever as a supreme threat to our freedom and, paradoxically, a simultaneous demonstration that our system worked the best.

But in less than two years, all of that changed. How could it have happened so fast, and why did so few of us see it coming? Lots of people were on record that it could not last *forever*, but no one that I know pinpointed the years of 1989–1990, or even the decade of decline, the 1980s; least among these our own Central Intelligence Agency.

The degree to which our "intelligence" agency missed the most important political change since World War II escaped much of the public notice it deserved. The record of CIA pronouncements shows that far from seeing a coming *demise*, the Agency believed as late as 1988 that the Soviet Union was economically viable, was producing about half as much material output as the United States, and was spending about 15 percent of its GNP on its military.

After the curtain fell, it became evident that the deterioration was so great that it had to have begun much earlier than 1989, probably as early as 1980, and that Soviet economic output was surely no more than a third that of the United States, maybe as little as a fourth. If so, then Soviet *military* expenditures in the late 1980s may have been exceeding 25 percent of Soviet GNP, a feat we ourselves have only been able to sustain for relatively short periods during wartime. If these revised assessments are correct, it should be of little surprise that the decline had been overdue and that the threat of Soviet world domination had been completely lame for several years.

How could an agency that spends billions of dollars on intelligence assessment and economic analysis have made such an error? With all the tools at its command, how could the world's largest team of intelligence experts have missed the size and structure of the Soviet economy by hundreds of billions of dollars?

The facts in this case are plain to see. The Iron Curtain fell in 1989 and no one predicted it. The Soviet economy was in near paralysis and no one in the U.S. government seemed to know it. CIA reports, in fact, suggested just the opposite.

The big point in terms of building our own intellectual capital is this: No one predicted the demise of communism the way it happened, at the time it happened, because *no one can predict or ever will be able to predict the future*. This truth is obvious, but cannot be overstated. We *wish* this were not so, and we officially commission people to go on predicting, with ever more sophisticated tools, but alas, the results are nil.

Some forecasters come closer to good predictions than others. These are almost always individuals or very small, eclectic groups, thinking independently and not highly regarded. Culturally, we prefer to trust the predictions of large, appointed groups, even though this nearly always prevents us from standing on firm ground. No place is solid, as Archimedes warned us, but some places are indeed much less solid than others, especially official forecasts.

The job of any individual intellect is as much to avoid the weak positions as to find strong ones. Above all, the individual intellect must resist the illusion of concreteness.

The collective intellect will not likely change its mind merely because of the outright failure of a principal institution. Perhaps even the opposite could happen—*more* money to the CIA, so that the next analysis will be more complete! Our language calls on us to have "Central Intelligence," and at a very deep level, therefore, we will always believe that the approach will work.

REAL KNOWLEDGE RESIDES IN THE SINGLE HUMAN MIND

What we are dealing with in the case of the World Bank is not the expansion of knowledge, but the expansion of information.

The "World Development Report 1988" does not contain what I would call knowledge. It does not contain a large stock of intellectual capital, but only a certain class of raw material that is not necessarily of the highest quality, for the encyclopedic style and the bureaucratic approval process have degraded the ore.

What we are also dealing with here, in the case both of the World Bank and the CIA, is the nature of complexity itself and its place in the universe. As time runs its course, the world does not become simpler and more unified, but much more complex and diversified. As physicist Freeman Dyson puts it, the universe is "infinite in all directions," and is becoming more so every day. Computer models, even the very large ones maintained by the CIA, are quickly overwhelmed by the actual scope of complexity in the real world.

In addition, we must understand the fact that the locus of knowledge is not in books, but in the minds of living individuals. In the case of the World Bank or the CIA, as with all other such institutions, its president or its director can speak for it administratively but not intellectually. In other words, no one in the Bank or the Agency understands everything about the institution's findings about the world. The best either bureaucracy can do is to publish a thick handbook in the pretense that we will all believe that this handbook proves that the Bank and the Agency have the kind of knowledge we all wish it did. Our wish is so strong that we are greatly surprised to find that it has not come true.

So what we are countering with here—strongly and irreverently, in the belief that this will help us build our own intellectual capital—is the view that the presence of an authoritative but impenetrable text implies the existence of someone, somewhere who is actually possessed of the knowledge that we imagine must be in such a text. We wish this were true. We wish that someone, somewhere really did understand the great problems of the day, but no single mind does. It is the single mind that is the very locus of intellectual capital itself.

SHOULD I OR SHOULD I NOT
READ THE EXPERTS?

And yet no need is greater than to understand the world, unless it is the ability to pass this understanding on to others. Now how would I answer the question, "Should I or should I not read the 'World Development Report 1988'?"

My answer is to treat it for what it is, a *handbook*—surely a unique one, perhaps even a good one, as handbooks go. If after such a recognition you want to "read" it, fine, but what will more likely happen is to read *in* it, for the parts that your own intellect seems to need for the puzzle it is currently assembling. The recognition that the book is a multiple authored report destined mainly for other multiple author teams in other institutions should help remove the guilt we all feel for not being able to read all of something whose subject is so clearly important and which, if we *could* digest it, would decidedly improve our world view. The World Bank will continue mainly administrating a stock of monetary capital; in large measure, however, we shall have to enhance our own intellectual capital elsewhere.

——10——

Breaking the Control
of Language
The Case of "Scientific Systems"

In highlighting the shortcomings of the World Bank and the Central Intelligence Agency, I take considerable risk. To say that something falls short of an ideal is often taken to mean that the thing is no good at all. In this chapter I will highlight the inadequacies, in terms of how they hamper the intellect, of the entire American culture, its language, its shortage of common sense, and especially its love of science.

The risk in this approach is that readers may initially feel that I am disrespectful of my native country and that I am forgetting the solid achievements to which the aforementioned institutions, let alone America itself, can certainly lay claim.

Unquestionably and without doubt, no better "system" exists than the American one. We may look all around but nowhere else on earth has any country achieved the level of material success that the United States has. The material success is so great, in fact, that our main problems have become what to do with surpluses rather than how to overcome shortages. In the United States we have an overabundance of food, automobiles, televisions, appliances, CD players, of virtually anything that can be said to constitute part of the "material standard of living." We have so many goods that we are busy building personal lockers and warehouses in the countryside to hold the stuff we can no longer cram into our homes in the city.

The big problem in America today, as I see it, is not failure but success. The questions we face are not about what to do to reverse our failures, but rather what to do next now that we have succeeded. It is in this context, in this praise of freedom and the material abundance it can bring, that I want to shine the irreverent light of reason on our culture. To move beyond material success, to seek a new level of overall peace and cultural serenity, we will require not only more knowledge of the kind we now have but even larger amounts of intellectual capital of a whole new class and quality.

In reaching for this new knowledge, we must see our culture, our language, and our science not only as the powerful tools of material success they surely are, but also as virtual "prisons" for the intellect that wants to break through to new vistas. To see through these walls of convention first requires careful if not minute inspection. To eventually be good at synthesis, we must have also spent significant time at analysis.

WHAT THE INTELLECT CANNOT DELEGATE

Let me begin with examples of two rather simple kinds of errors embedded in our culture and language, to illustrate the kinds of "prisons" we must learn to burst. Then I will proceed to a third, more important problem: the edifice of error supporting our unquestioning faith in science.

A photo in a magazine advertisement shows a wealthy man in his sixties taking a phone call in his foyer while his wife is waiting impatiently by the front door, ready to leave for a social occasion. The caption of the ad is, "Should you try to manage a $15 million portfolio on your own?" The sponsor of the ad is a large New York bank that offers private investment management. The automatic answer many of us have to the ad's question is, "No, I'd better have an expert do it."

In my view, however, the right answer to the question, "Should you try to manage a $15 million portfolio on your own" is this: "Since you have no choice, yes you should." In other words, there really is no way out of managing the portfolio yourself, regardless of its size. To turn investments over to an investment manager is to decide to manage the manager rather than the investments directly. Since no such hired manager can reliably predict markets any better than you can, you are left to manage both the manager and the portfolio. The crux of the error is the *wish* that someone (a "professional") really could predict the direction of investment markets, which no one can, along with the associated error of "ought to be able": If anyone *ought to be able* to manage investments well, it *ought* to be the big banks because they have more investments than anyone. Even though banks, by definition, ought to know how to do it, they do not.

So strong is our cultural predilection to believe in how things ought to work that many readers will no doubt have come this far without remembering the banking fiascos of the 1980s and early 1990s, in which the Third World debt crisis and the U.S. Savings and Loan crisis have destroyed hundreds of institutions and ruined millions of investors, let alone the apparently random gyrations of the stock and bond markets, in which 5 or 10 percent of an issue's value can disappear in a day for reasons no one can exactly pinpoint—even after Congressional investigation.

The lesson in this case is that the intellect has no way out of responsibility for gaining knowledge about the world and its ways; the intellect cannot turn this responsibility for knowing things better than other people over to other people. If it does so, it risks severe peril.

Another advertisement in a magazine shows a digitized aerial view of a coastal city and its surrounding farmland from a hundred miles up. The caption says, "Our data helps investors

Truth

One of the main reasons the surplus of information today strikes us as so overwhelming is the attitude we have about truth. Likewise, one of the principal reasons we so strongly revere experts is our belief that they are persons who can ascertain truth, in the sense of absolute, Newtonian certainty. Our attitude is that sufficient study of "all the facts" will yield the "truth" about what we should do next, in business and even in politics. We treat the most tangled and extended of situations—the Iran-Contra Affair or the Savings and Loan Crisis—as though the actors were causal billiard balls on a smooth table, who respond to direct taps at discrete angles, and we appoint commissions to "get to the bottom" of millions of individual aspirations, motivations, delusions, and mistakes as though they were cumulative products of the laws of physics. We are always somewhat disappointed when the consensus of an expert panel is fuzzy, or when the experts cannot even form a consensus, but this does not deter us a day later from appointing another tribunal to investigate our next embarrassing political snafu.

Our common law itself demands truth of the absolute kind, that every crime be causally linked to a guilty party with clear but illegal motivations. I once testified in a case of business law in which the plaintiff alleged that the corporation for which I had worked, six years earlier, had failed to pay a proper fee for real estate advice that the corporation later allegedly adopted as a profitable strategy. As I answered counsel's questions, I referred to my old file of memoranda, maps, and spreadsheets, but I kept thinking, "What do these *prove*?" My memory of the living corporate atmosphere six years previously was, "In those days, we weren't sure what to do," "We couldn't figure it out," "We didn't know whether to expand or not," "We argued and changed our mind a dozen times," "The executive VP pushed for it out of a power play," "A new competitor appeared ready to do it if we didn't," and "It was a toss-up, but we finally went ahead after two years, so we could stop worrying about it." Neither the lawyers nor the judge were interested in my ruminations about how cloudy the decision really was and how little a particular piece of outside advice could have meant. What they wanted were simple, direct answers. To them, corporations all have formal strategic plans to make profits, which they relentlessly implement, in point-to-point logic. They saw it as straightforward cause and effect, and they wanted truth with a capital "T."

Culturally, we do not accept the relativity of knowledge and truth, but only their absoluteness. We believe in the existence of "right answers." We think in terms of "sound investment advice" as though it can be purchased at a high enough price. But the fact that some advisers are sounder than others does not mean that they are right absolutely, only that they are slightly (ever so slightly!) righter than their competitors.

This is the proper attitude we should adopt about truth. It is not possible to ascertain truth with a capital "T," but it is possible to come minutely closer to it, or to achieve it sooner than your competition.

---

make crop yield predictions for use in market forecasts." The sponsor of the ad is a company that launches satellites.

The correct reaction, in my opinion, to this claim, "Our data helps investors make crop yield predictions for use in market forecasts," is twofold. First of all, people do not *invest* in commodity markets, they *trade* them (they speculate). Second, crop yield predictions by whatever method, on the ground or overhead, are almost always wrong. On top of this, the only predictions that move the commodity markets are the official forecasts of government agencies, such as the Agriculture Department. And last, markets are not always moved by the government's figures themselves; markets see every day many more than one aspect of supply and demand; therefore, the possibility exists that on the day of a new government crop yield forecast, there may easily be other more important information coming into the market: a riot in the former Soviet Union, a war in the Persian Gulf, an enormous sale of gold in an associated market, and so forth.

The aforementioned ad, sponsored by a scientific company, represents what its engineers *wish* was true, that markets (and other human affairs) could be seen from space. However, our affairs are much too complex for instruments of this kind. Data have to do with small parts of our past and never reveal the future neatly and automatically, the way we all wish.

In both of these cases, we see the cultural wish for an easier way of knowing things than by applying our intelligence directly. We wish that experts could know things for us, but they do not. We wish that machines and high technology could know things for us, but they also cannot. In both of these cases, we see the role of language in protecting cultural myth. Is not a "bank" something we can "trust"? Is not a "satellite" a "spy in the sky"?

OUR LOVE AFFAIR WITH "SCIENTIFIC SYSTEMS"

Is Nature Predictable?

In the past few years, a small number of established scientists have begun to speak of the indeterminacy of certain natural processes. In other words, these scientists acknowledge that some things may exist that science will not ever be capable of fully understanding or predicting. They do not make this admission willingly, or with genuine humility, but as a concession to reality—a concession that no doubt, most of them hope is temporary.

One prominent example of such unpredictability is the weather, or as it is known in the longer term, climate. We can all see from personal experience that weather cannot be predicted; we know first hand that a forecast for sunshine two days hence cannot reliably be used to plan an outdoor picnic free of a downpour. We routinely choose to ignore this simple truth, however, and assume that scientists are hard at work on the weather prediction problem and that they will gradually make progress. We hold this assumption despite the fact that progress has been very, very slow. In the past four decades, weather forecasts have advanced in accuracy by less than one day. Forty years ago, in 1950, a forecast of what the weather would be in 48 hours had only a 50–50 chance of being right; today, the accuracy of a forecast reverts to 50–50 at about 60 hours into the future.

Our Love of Forecasts and Belief in Trends

The amazing thing about our culture, however, is that we listen eagerly, day after day, to the next such forecast and to the next one after that as though each new one had a decidedly better chance of being right than the last one. And even more truly amazing is that we listen attentively, again and again, to long-range climate forecasts for the year 2050 as though the "science of climatology" deserved our complete credence, despite the fact that its short-term sister, the "science of meteorology," becomes useless only two and one-half days into the future.

The question that common sense should ask immediately is, "How can predictive tools that do not work for a period of several days be any more reliable for a period of several decades?" Most people, however, do not raise this objection. Instead, they seem to see the world as a large, well-behaved system that ought to be predictable, especially in a general sense over a long period of time. They admit that you cannot predict the time and place of a specific thunderstorm, but they believe that you can (or ought to be able to) predict the overall trends.

One recent attest to this belief was the sale of 8 million copies of the book *Megatrends*. The sales came not so much from Naisbitt's actually perceiving the right trends (he did not do so, of course) as from his coining the term, "megatrends," which neatly affirmed that such things should exist.

The process by which the mass intellect makes such an error deserves our careful attention, and I shall try to demonstrate it not so much in scientific terms as in linguistic and cultural terms. My method will be to concentrate on the power and the limits of a single word.

Nonlinear Systems

Let's go back now to the scientists who admit that they cannot predict everything, of which climate is a good example of something that is inherently indeterminate. Peter V. Foukal, a solar physicist and president of Cambridge Research and Instrumentation, Inc., makes the admission as follows:

> Is it realistic to expect that astronomers will ever be able to make long-term predictions about the behavior of the sun? There may be fundamental restrictions on the possibility of such predictions if the processes driving the solar cycle are nonlinear. Nonlinear systems do not behave in the predictable manner of simple oscillators, such as a pendulum; relatively straightforward feedback of an "effect" on its "cause" can lead to bewilderingly complex behavior. Even when their behavior is governed by a well-understood set of forces, nonlinear oscillators can be so sensitive to initial conditions that predictions extending substantially into the future become impossible. (*Scientific American,* February 1990, p. 41)

This may be as close to a confession of the "limits of science" as we are ever likely to see, although it is by no means an unconditional surrender. Instead of raising a plain white flag, Schneider deploys special, scientific language. He uses the terms, "nonlinear systems" and "nonlinear oscillators." This relieves him of having to say candidly that "climate behaves in ways that are impossible for us to fathom."

Foukal says instead, "If the processes driving the solar cycle are nonlinear," then predictions become impossible. He might perhaps have said, "If the processes driving the solar

cycle are unpredictable, then predictions become impossible."
But he did not say it this way because he wanted to emphasize
the special word, "nonlinear," and he wanted to preserve the
overall concept of "system." It would not ring true in our ears
if he had said that the solar cycle is an "unpredictable system." It sounds better for a scientist to say that it is a "nonlinear system" that is impossible to predict. You get the
impression that whatever "nonlinear" is, maybe one day we can
crack it.

All Systems Are Predictable

Actually, in the world of science, an "unpredictable system" is a
contradiction in terms. Nothing that can rightly be called a "system" is unpredictable. Any true system will eventually become
fully understood. It does not matter what modifier is used:
"complex system," "large system," "nonlinear system," and so
on. If a thing is indeed a system, then its workings are regular,
and they will ultimately be found to be logical.

It is the word "system," then, and our permissiveness in
using it to label whatever we wish, that is the true culprit here—
the intellectual error that so often and forcefully sidetracks our
mind.

As I address this linguistic trap in more and more detail, I
am fully aware that many readers may say, "Please come back
up to the surface. You're in too deep!"

But I urge this part of my audience to pause and take a deep
breath so that we can zoom the microscope down even more
finely: What I want to show is a view inside the prison of language. I want to show how a single word ("system") limits the
range of our thought and to suggest the immense possibilities
that lie beyond, once we become conscious of the faulty use of a
word and begin to search for better ways of expression.

In correct usage, the word "system" is inseparable from the
word "design." The existence of a system implies the existence
of a designer. A system is designed to meet goals and objectives

Imperfectionism

The Big Bang Theory holds that the universe began suddenly some 13 billion years ago. Before the Big Bang, all of the matter in the universe was in one place. At the moment of the Big Bang, all of the matter in the universe "exploded," i.e., it began a rapid, enormous expansion that is still continuing today.

The main problem with the Big Bang Theory is something that astronomers refer to as "lumpiness." Everywhere we look in the distant skies, we see "lumps" of matter: planets, galaxies, and "walls" of galaxies. The patterns in which universal matter now arrays itself are not only far-flung but complex and unique. The question is, How did these patterns happen?

How could it be that at one moment the matter of the universe was uniform and at the next moment it was heading outward in nonuniform lumps?

The problem is further complicated by the fact that the main force in the universe, gravity, appears today to be very smooth and uniform. In other words, gravity, left to itself, would have produced a very regular, even distribution of matter, and not the irregular clusters, pockets, and clumps we see today.

A scientist at Princeton, however, recently came up with a computer model which he says solves the problem. According to J. Richard Gott, an astrophysics professor, the force of gravity will indeed explain today's shape of the universe, IF you make one simple assumption.

If you assume that in the very first fraction of a second of the Big Bang there were random fluctuations (Gott calls them "extremely faint wrinkles"), then gravity is sufficient to explain all of today's resulting "lumps."

So the key to the design of the universe, according to the latest in astrophysics, is imperfection.

It is amusing to think that we can go around making grand assumptions with computers about the necessary imperfections in the structure of the universe and yet, at the same time, expect that our own affairs, and indeed the affairs of the entire world community, should proceed with perfection.

I wonder if we would not all benefit from taking the astronomers' view of imperfection: that it is not so much a "flaw" as a "design secret." The idea would be to shift more toward an attitude of tolerance for the nature of things as opposed to a rigid goal of overly perfecting them.

---

and connotes a measure of efficiency and maximization. When a company announces a new "health care system," we expect it to be a carefully selected set of benefits and eligibility rules designed to maximize care while minimizing overall cost to the group and the company. We know that such a system will have been designed in committee and will have been subject to an extensive "trade-off analysis," and so we will not be truly surprised to discover, perhaps later on, that the system was not well designed. "Some system," we might say. "It covers false teeth but not appendicitis."

The problem here, however, is not so much with the fact that humans design lots of second-rate systems, but rather that we apply the ideal concept of a perfect system to things that have evolved rather than having actually ever been designed. For instance, we may speak of "the international banking system" or even "the system of democratic capitalism." Both of these things are *like* what we mean by a system, in the word's ideal sense, but no overall human designer has been at work (not even a committee), and the behavior of both banking and democracy is so complex, messy, and chaotic as to defy any implication of being truly "systematic."

But Is Everything a System?

Let us ask now a series of questions, not so much to set the stage for a grand *answer,* but to illustrate how we throw around labels without considering the full consequences.

For instance, is nature a "system"? Perhaps the finest system ever designed? If so, who was the designer? Does nature have a magnificent blueprint? If so, what were the designer's goals and objectives? Or is nature something that has merely evolved and in its tangled complexity gives the appearance of being systematic? Do all systems, regardless of their designers, have "flaws," such as tornados, hurricanes, earthquakes, volcanoes, and meteorites? Are such flaws a deliberate part of the design? Did the designer perform a trade-off analysis? Do natural systems have limits? Is a natural system designed to do one set of things but not another?

What do you call something which, if it has been designed, has been partly designed by evolution and natural selection? Or if the design is sacred, who has the right to change the design? Who has enough knowledge or wisdom to change it? Is not changing it actually the same as redesigning it? Can you help from changing it? Do you vote against some design changes and not others? Is it okay to change it if you mean well? Do you attempt to preserve the design, insofar as you can see it, without change? Why? Has not the design changed markedly on its own over the past four billion years?

Are humans a part of the system design or a flaw? Is technology a design feature that humankind has simply uncovered, a means to tap other features that were hidden, for its comfort and sustenance? Which technologies are natural, which are not—fire but not nuclear fire?

Is the science of humankind a discipline that can and will disclose the full design principles of nature and the universe? Are those scientists who today speak of nonlinear systems (unpredictable systems) merely unsuccessful at their work?

Or must we find a way to speak of our universe that is more imaginative than comparing it to a "system"? What if the universe is more complicated than we think it to be? What if the universe, in fact, is even more complicated than we can imagine it to be? Won't our knowledge and the fruits of such knowledge be all the greater if we break out of the prison of applying "scientific systems analysis" to everything, as though the whole world and its societies and cultures were a giant Swiss watch with intermeshing gears?

The reader may well think at this point that I want science completely banished. This, of course, is not so. In fact, I would not mind more science, if it were applied to the domain of science, by which I mean such things as machines, materials, and electronics.

What I want the most is an acknowledgment that, outside of its domain, it is science that has the inherent limits, not nature, not the earth, not the universe, and not even necessarily mankind and the human intellect.

Onset of "Big Science" to Study "Big Systems"

At the present time, however, I am well removed from having what I want. In *The New York Times* of June 17, 1990, we find a discussion of the pros and cons of NASA's $30 billion "Earth Observing System" (EOS), which the agency wants to have in place by the year 2000. "The Earth and its atmosphere make up a single, seamless, interdependent system," says journalist William K. Stevens, and EOS "will supply the means for the first time, to monitor and measure on a global scale many of the complex interactions of air, sea, land and living things that create and manipulate the climate."

My point is this: Stevens is wrong. The earth is not a system. The earth is also not an "ecosystem." Especially it is not a system the design of which scientists can uncover with $30 billion. The earth is something much more complex than a NASA team can imagine, let alone attempt to fully measure and then redesign.

Implications of Systems Design (or Redesign)

It is the redesign implied in our undertaking of large science projects that should bother us the most, because to execute any

―――――― ◇ ――――――

Simplicity

To simplify something means to make it less complex and intricate. But simplicity is much harder to achieve than complexity, and in this sense simplicity is itself very complex.

The mind, of course, simplifies things spontaneously, without our consciously telling it to do so. In fact, without simplification, life would cease. In a world of ever-expanding diversity, we must all make simplifications, or we could not take another step.

There is a distinction, however, between simplification and oversimplification. In other words, there is right simplification, and there is error. The highest form of right simplification, the kind of thing we recognize when we see it because it reshapes so many of our existing ideas and connections, is elegance.

The achieving of right simplification requires great appreciation of, and tolerance for, complexity. The longer you can dwell in chaos before quickly oversimplifying something, the better chance you have of pulling it together rightly.

――――――――――――――――――――

redesign implies a change in politics toward central control and away from individual freedom. We should not look forward to a systems analysis of something that is not a system to tell us to change our entire way of life in order to better fit a perceived system design (or redesign).

That which we wish to limit we first call a system. The demand then arises for rapid knowledge of the system's design, followed by its redesign to eliminate "flaws" or reach "higher objectives." Execution of the redesign implies central control by those who believe they are smart enough to comprehend it all, that is, by those who did the systems study. What a system we then have!

The American System

A friend of mine who is a native Australian has lived in the United States for the past 20 years, and although he would not say that our approach is perfect, he agrees that it works better than all the others. What he says about it fits well with the aforementioned ideas on misuse of the word "system": "The American system works well," my friend says, "because its doesn't work too well."

This is precisely the kind of distinction we must make about systems and "systems science" in order to most powerfully enhance our individual stocks of intellectual capital.

11

Challenging the Latest Scholarship

The Case of "Global Warming"

THE MEANING OF
WORLD-CLASS SCHOLARSHIP

When I was a student of literature in the 1950s at The University of Kansas, I had one professor who was a world-recognized scholar. His name was Dr. Charlton Hinman and his field was Shakespeare. What had made Dr. Hinman famous, over the course of several decades of study in British libraries, was the invention of a special "collating machine" by which detailed, side-by-side comparisons could be made of Shakespeare's various original texts, and Hinman's use of this machine to discover (or so he claimed) that the first printed folios of Shakespeare had been set not by four typographers but by five. In the 1600s, each typographer exercised a degree of judgment on spelling and word choice which today is reserved only for chief editors and which in fact would certainly require an author's approval before printing. But the typographers in Shakespeare's time had great latitude, there being as yet no dictionaries of the correct meanings and spellings of words. Hinman showed that the fifth typographer may have made important changes in many of the plays' key lines upon which we depend to know, for instance, whether Hamlet was truly suicidal or Lear truly mad. These kinds of judgments about characters, in turn, govern our overall view of Shakespeare's outlook on humankind (his *weltan-schauung*), whether it is essentially dark and pessimistic or vice versa.

An amusing recollection, you may be thinking, but hardly of any importance to the world of scholarship today—or to the real world of the twentieth century. Today, major judgments are made with full access to the facts and with much greater certainty than in the past, because of our advances in science and logic.

HOW CLOSE CAN WE COME TO TRUTH?

Whereas I am generally disposed to believe in the idea of human progress, I would like to build the case here that nothing much has changed about scholarship, that (in all fields) it still depends crucially on the comparison and verification of texts and that we are in no degree closer to certainty of judgment about major elements of our affairs than centuries ago.

In fact, it seems to me that one of the big problems for the future is our naive belief that truth can be discovered, that experts are the ones who know what it is, and that society should put their expert findings to work for the betterment of humankind and the world.

The first objection to this belief is the one we have heard again and again, but that we have nonetheless not accepted, neither in law nor politics. The scale of information and misinformation today makes it impossible for anyone to know all the important facts of a case. For instance, according to the Librarian of Congress, the documentary evidence under his care concerning the Iran-Contra affair now occupies over 10,000 two-cubic-foot boxes and requires merely for its electronic index several reels of magnetic computer tape. The question is, Whom do we think is capable of digesting and accurately judging this mass of evidence? An expert? A jury? An honest lawyer? A journalist reporting to the public?

The second objection to the belief about humankind's ability to ascertain truth, and to modify its behavior accordingly, has to do with a key operating procedure of science, namely the ability to replicate. In other words, the way we know whether or not a reported scientific principle is true or not is that we repeat the experiment that is said to prove it. If hundreds or thousands of scientists can replicate a procedure, and/or if the procedure leads to a device, a compound, or something else of physical worth, then we can conclude with reasonable sureness that the principle involved has a high degree of truth, or at least has a high degree of practical efficacy.

But back to the 10,000 boxes of information on Iran-Contra. Suppose someone did spend the time (years or more) to master all the details, and suppose this expert now makes a pronouncement about what the data means and who is guilty and who is not. How can such an investigation be replicated? Is any expert so completely competent and trustworthy that we need not check his or her conclusions? How can a jury decide that the expert's multiyear analysis is right or wrong?

One of the biggest problems in the 1990s is that the public will have to act as jury over an increasing number of vast "scientific" studies that multiple experts cannot replicate and that do not result in machines or compounds but in recommendations for changing our way of life, sometimes completely changing our way of life.

CAN WE MAKE DETERMINATIONS ONCE AND FOR ALL?

The best current example of this situation is the warning from some scientists that we must soon forego the use of fossil fuels in order to combat global warming caused by the greenhouse effect. To forego fossil fuels, or severely to restrict them, means essentially to change everything about modern life. And indeed, some advocates say, unabashedly, "Yes, it's back to bicycles."

By now the public is perhaps modestly aware that there is dissension about global warming, that at least some of the experts disagree. But even if such awareness does exist, our prevailing mood is for the experts to get on with it quickly, to make the measurements that may be needed, and to decide the thing one way or the other and take action.

In an article in the August 1990 *Scientific American*, Philip D. Jones and Tom M. L. Wigley, both of the University of East Anglia in Norwich, England, say that they have completed a ten-year study "to collect and analyze, once and for all, every available historical temperature record" (p. 84). Result: The world has gotten warmer over the past century by one-half degree Centigrade. Humankind must immediately formulate and implement policies to reduce temperature increases caused by greenhouse gases. "The longer the world waits to act, the greater will be the climate change that future generations will have to endure" (p. 84).

Before we write Congress for action, let's consider in more detail what Jones and Wigley claim to have done in their ten-year study, and whether—on general grounds, quite apart from their good academic reputations—we should accept their conclusion and change our entire way of life.

THE MEANING OF WORLD-CLASS CLIMATOLOGY

Jones and Wigley gathered and analyzed 3,000 sets of temperature records, consisting of every available scrap of evidence they could find on the temperature of various places on earth since records began. Early records were kept by climate enthusiasts, who may sometimes have been educated scientists, but who were not under the control and standardization of any public authority. The first job for Jones and Wigley was to toss out records that had obvious errors in calculations, such as mistakes in the averaging of monthly means. They also tossed out temperature series for a given station in which the actual measurement site was moved over time, inasmuch as moving uphill could bias the record toward colder, and downhill warmer. More elaborate procedures were needed to "patch" an area's temperature from one decade to the next, as in the case of a particular station's ceasing its operation, and another station, perhaps ten miles away, coming on line.

Other problems confronted by Jones and Wigley were that early in the recorded history of temperature, by which we mean the 1800s, no measurements are available for the vast interiors of Africa, Asia, South America, and Australia. Temperature records for the Arctic and Antarctic (critical areas, by the way, as they contain the ice that Jones and Wigley fear will melt) are limited because early mercury thermometers froze. Over the past century the thermometer itself has been constantly redesigned and "improved." Furthermore, for most of the past century, only scattered measurements are available over the world's oceans, which cover two-thirds of the earth's surface and which were taken by vessels at irregular intervals and at imprecisely known locations. Temperature measurements taken close to the ocean's surface by an early sailing ship would be different from those measurements taken today atop the superstructure of the QEII. Water temperature ascertained from a bucket over the side is different from water temperature taken through an inlet valve well below the surface, as is now common practice. Another of the hundreds of problems in verifying all these old texts is that most recording stations on land were in or near cities, all of which grew in population and got warmer due to the well-acknowledged "heat island" effect. But do urban records give trustworthy information on the overall atmosphere itself?

WHO CHECKS THE CHECKERS?

Despite these difficulties and hundreds more, Jones and Wigley, in much the same way as my Shakespeare professor, say they have considered all the problems in the data, have made all the right judgments about what to exclude and what not to exclude, and have thus presented us with the authoritative version of world temperature history from 1850 to 1990. The question is, Who, without also spending the ten years, can replicate their work and verify their judgment? In the case of whether Shakespeare was typeset by five people or four, we might certainly agree to skip additional effort, because the results do not seem to be "earth-shaking." But what are we to do about the record of the world's temperature? Upon whom do we rely to verify the two experts from the University of East Anglia? Perhaps some other university such as MIT, some of whose climatologists have put forward a different series than Jones and Wigley, showing *no* change in world ocean temperature for 120 years, could replicate the study. Or perhaps NASA (still under suspicion for mistakenly putting a flawed billion-dollar telescope in space) could attempt it.

The general question of what to do about nonreplicable data from experts is a big problem for the 1990s—especially with a public who likes its evidence simplified and dramatized, who believes that the merits of a case always win out (no matter whose money is controlling the PR levers), and who, oddly enough (considering the success of American individualism), has a yearning for rapid and decisive leadership on complex issues by elected officials in a position to exercise central control.

IS IRREVERENCE FOR SCHOLARS IMPOLITE?

At the core of this issue is our increasing inability to trust common sense and simple analysis, our readiness to have others think for us, and our reverence for academic study. Despite the fact that we can call our present educational system a "complete mess," our admiration for academics remains so great that we are incapable of dismissing what they tell us on the simple grounds that it sounds silly. This would be irreverent (impolite), and our culture demands respect for recognized experts, mainly on the basis of credentials rather than verifiable results.

In the case of global warming, the scare is based on several severe violations of common sense:

1. How can a process (climate) that is millions of years long be understood from the records of the past 140 years, regardless of the records' authenticity?

2. On the other hand, assuming that the 140-year record is indeed valid, revealing a half degree Celsius rise in global temperature over its entire length, what do we make of the intermediate period, from 1940 to about 1975, when the average temperature actually *cooled?* What forces were at work for those 35 years? Humankind must have been busy beginning to warm things, was it not, so the cooling must have been natural—and if so, why not again in the next few decades?

3. Is it not a trifle arrogant to assume that humankind, by its very presence, now overwhelms the natural climatic forces that produced glaciers, ice ages, and mountain ranges?

TAKING OWNERSHIP OF INTERPRETATION

Finally, in rediscovering the reigns of our own ability to think independently, we must remember that those who compile and put order to natural data are not automatically the best interpreters of what the data means. The closing argument of Jones and Wigley for changing our entire way of life to cure global warming is as follows: "A policy of inaction would be justified only if researchers were sure that the greenhouse effect was negligible." Researchers, of course, are not sure of this, nor will they ever be. As mentioned earlier, researchers do not understand why a cooling occurred from 1940 to 1975, and many researchers in the mid-1970s predicted that the earth was headed rapidly back into the ice ages. Furthermore, researchers today are not sure what the results of their global warming forecasts would bring, whether good or bad.

The one thing, however, upon which all researchers agree and which we the public eagerly support (with billions of dollars in research grants) is that researchers should be in control of major policy decisions. "Let us make policy," we are fond of saying, "on the basis of sound scientific findings, not on mere emotion." This naive view of the potential of science outside its domain is a fundamental weakness of twentieth-century culture which will continue to constrain our progress in the coming decade.

—————12—————

Objecting to "Popular Religion"

The Case of Environmentalist Wendell Berry

LISTENING CAREFULLY TO
OUR ADVERSARIES

In the fall of 1989, my wife, my daughters, and I spent the Thanksgiving holidays with my mother in southern Missouri. On the Friday after Thanksgiving, the women went shopping and I had a full day to spend at the public library in Joplin. This was a rare privilege in a busy life, and I approached the friendly, open stacks and the comfortable wooden chairs and large tables in a joyous, energetic mood. "Now's the chance," I thought, "to get caught up on everything and to learn something new!"

The compulsion I have always felt in a library is to read all of it, or at least to put much more on my tray than I can possibly digest. This automatic reaction to a feast, however, has tempered somewhat in midlife, because of the practicality we gradually learn and because of the peace we begin to make with our own ignorance. In addition, there is the recognition that, completely within the confines of any single library today, documentary evidence can be found to support virtually any proposition we might care to make, as well as its antithesis.

112

Nonetheless, in the Joplin library in 1989, I set myself the goal of launching a major project that I had long been contemplating; listing the principal environmental writers, identifying their main works, reading them, noting their key arguments, finding the commonalities, and then finally of holding this framework up to the light of reason before reassessing my own conclusions. The names on my list included Paul Ehrlich, James Lovelock, Jeremy Rifkin, Bill McKibben, John McPhee, Barry Commoner, Wendell Berry, Lester Brown, and some others perhaps less well known.

All of us as students are encouraged to be objective, and none of us wants to be accused of not listening to the facts. But as time goes on, we all have greater and greater difficulty in honestly listening to our adversaries. We have been over the ground before, have come down on one side or another, and have proceeded on our own direction in life—and to open up a clean, clear channel to persons with whom we are very likely to disagree is not only distasteful, it is very hard work. "Your adversary is never completely wrong," a friend of mine says, and I know that if I listen carefully enough to my opponents, I will have to sharpen and modify my own views, if not significantly change them.

MY INTRODUCTION TO "LIMITS"

A complete change of mind is, of course, the hardest work of all. As a much younger man and an unthinking enthusiast for technology and perpetual human progress, I read *The Limits to Growth*, published by The Club of Rome in 1972. The findings of this study, perhaps the first to use computer-driven models of the future, kept me depressed for many years, until about 1980, when the market itself showed that the price of crude oil and other raw materials can indeed decline and when the antithesis to *Limits* finally began to appear in published works, most notably Herman Kahn's *The Coming Boom* and Julian Simon's *The*

Ultimate Resource. With the help of these authors, I gained enough skepticism to challenge both the data and the methods of *Limits,* and to arrive at a more positive view of our future. By the mid-1980s, I came to support the basic proposition that human imagination is our only true limit and that the human species, therefore, is not automatically doomed to an early end by what appears to some as "finite resources."

What I sought to do in the library in Joplin in 1989 was, at least partly, to retest my view, but (I'm sure) mainly to discover new means by which to defeat the opposition and to win people over to a more optimistic outlook of humanity's future. I did not, of course, complete my goal that Thanksgiving of reading the entire universe of environmentalist writings, but I did carefully read and annotate several of the writers, including McPhee, McKibben, and Berry. I rediscovered the notes of this encounter in a desk file called "environmentalist theory" when a friend wrote me about my view of Wendell Berry.

"Wendell Berry is tackling many of the same issues as you, though from a rather different perspective," the friend said. "I'd be interested in knowing the degree to which your perspective and his might mesh." A copy of Berry's "Out of Your Car, Off Your Horse," from the February 1991 *Atlantic* was enclosed. The subtitle of the article was "Twenty-seven Propositions about Global Thinking and the Sustainability of Cities."

THE TROUBLE WITH "MOTHER AND APPLE PIE"

The earlier article, the one I had studied in 1989, was from a commencement address given by Berry in Bar Harbor, Maine, called "The Futility of Global Thinking." The way I summarized his point of view in my notes is as follows:

> We all live by robbing nature, parasitically. In making things always bigger and more centralized, we make them both more vulnerable in themselves and more dangerous to everything else.

Only petroleum (fossil fuel) permits this, because we are not smart enough or conscious enough or alert enough to work responsibly on a gigantic scale. There is no way out, because the world has finite resources. We must all achieve the moral character and acquire the skills to live at a much poorer material standard than we do today. Good possibilities exist at the local, community level, for persons with love. But this has not been well examined; we are locked into the wrong economy by (1) the greed of corporate stockholders, (2) the hubris of corporate executives, and (3) our addiction to cheap, plentiful energy.

The more recent article, "Out of Your Car, Off Your Horse," contains the same themes as the aforementioned, with perhaps more emphasis on the need of saving our dying planet, the impossibility of thinking globally, the unsustainability of our cities, and the need for action at the local level based on affection for people and place.

The big problem in tackling Berry is in seeming to declare against morality. Berry is solidly entrenched in rural America, reinforced by love and affection. Who can be against this? Who can say we need less love, less of the Golden Rule, less self-sufficiency, less small-scale technology, and more central planning and control? Who can say that we should forget about removing greed and pride from the conduct of human affairs? And who can say that, based on present conditions, we have successfully learned how to "think globally" and to apply such thought to the betterment of our affairs?

The question I have about Berry is not to dispute the value he puts on rural American morality but rather, How much of rural America is there to go around, and who gets it?

Berry says in the recent *Atlantic* article: "Some cities can never be sustainable, because they do not have a countryside around them, or near them, from which they can be sustained. New York City cannot be made sustainable, nor can Phoenix. Some cities in Kentucky or the Midwest, on the other hand, might reasonably hope to become sustainable."

HOW CAN WE EXPAND KENTUCKY?

My question is about the scope of this solution. How many of us can fit in Kentucky and the Midwest? If New York City and Phoenix are not sustainable, neither are Los Angeles, San Francisco, Denver, Detroit, Boston, Toronto, Edmonton, or Mexico City, London, Moscow, Tokyo, Cairo . . . where would we stop? Of the world's five billion people, two-thirds or more live in what Berry would call "unsustainable" cities; they have outgrown their countryside, or they have burgeoned (let's say in the case of Riyadh or Phoenix) in locales that were never meant to have a population of any size because of soil and climate. Only fossil fuels, Berry would say, permit cities to exist in the midst of inhospitable deserts; food and other necessities are trucked in, a process that is destroying the planet.

The town where Berry lives, however, Port Royal, Kentucky, is not presently sustainable either. The residents rely on electricity from many miles away, on gasoline from further, on fresh vegetables and fruit from Florida and South America, on meat from Iowa packers, on bread from large bakeries in Lexington, and so on. If Berry's approach were adopted, then grain, bread, and meat might be produced locally, but not vegetables and fruits, except for limited varieties seasonally, and except for what could be preserved through canning and freezing, provided energy were available for appliances.

We all have a longing for a "return" to the simpler life, but when we picture this kind of existence, we involuntarily coat it with sentimental sugar. We forget why our forefathers struggled so desperately to escape such an existence in the past. We forget about hospitals and clean, well-lighted operating rooms, with medical specialists and high tech equipment when we need them. We forget about the 25-year increase in longevity we have today, compared to a century ago when we all lived in mainly rural, self-sufficient settings. We forget that food poisoning is no longer a major concern in our daily lives, and we ignore the role of our marvelously varied diet (with lettuce salads and fruit affordable every day of the year) in improving our health and extending our lifetimes.

But if Berry is right, it won't last. The cities previously named and hundreds more will perish. The survivors will inhabit the countryside, or the naturally hospitable parts of the countryside. Globally, this means mainly the American Midwest, the Argentine Pampas, some parts of Europe, the southern Ukraine, the river valleys of India, the southern part of China, and a few small toeholds in Japan and Formosa. The surviving world, if we take Berry literally, will number in the millions, not in the billions.

THE FRONTIER OF THOUGHT-ACTION

Let me be the first to agree that today's world is not perfect. But is it really as bad as Berry believes? Do we really have firm evidence that present civilization is on a path to sure destruction, supported only by chance deposits of fossil fuels in the earth's crust? Are we certain that our imagination will fail to uncover other sources of energy in the coming decades, such as clean nuclear fusion or direct photoelectric conversion of solar radiation? Doesn't our record of technological achievement, whether it arose with the help of fossil fuels or not, give us a fighting chance of continued material prosperity?

What I most dispute with Berry is the idea that the planet is dying and that we are best advised to give up our cities *now*, head for the countryside, and develop the abilities we will need to survive at a much lower standard of living. In my view, it is not a solution warranted by history or by the facts about our environment today. Furthermore, it is a drastic solution that would work for only 1 of each 1,000 of us. Finally, it is a solution that distracts from the job of spreading wealth further and more evenly around the world, by means of trade, to the three billion people who desperately want the material success Berry so dislikes.

Material Abundance

As the 1990s proceed, as material abundance piles up and spreads to more parts of the world, and as markets become ever more diverse, the job of getting closer to the "truth" than competitors becomes more and more challenging. The reason for this is that, in an age of overabundance, politics and culture (mass psychology) play a larger role in business decisions. In an age of scarcity, when people are short of basic goods, they behave more economically than psychologically. For instance, when people are short of food, they want to know mainly about the price and availability of what you have to offer. But when people have a surplus of food, as in America today, they want to know not only price and delivery but a host of other things: quality and freshness, nutritional profile, cholesterol content (by "good" and "bad" types), and how the food may have been produced, "artificially" or "naturally" (with or without fertilizer and chemicals). In this kind of buyers' market, business has fewer solid places on which to stand; not only must it figure consumer psychology into the price of *finished* goods, but also into the price of raw materials—lest a trade embargo of, say, South Africa (or California!), cut off a critical material or treble its price.

The dictum remains, however, that "your adversary is never completely wrong," and I want to affirm this in Berry's case. He is not wrong about the difficulty of "global thinking." Just as I personally did not conquer the Joplin library in a day, neither has anyone else. And Berry is also not wrong to urge us more in the direction of such moral qualities as love and affection. The very frontier of thought is its intersection with such moral qualities as honesty, courage, patience, and love.

At the same time, however, neither end of the mind-to-heart spectrum can be perfected. Berry says, "We are not smart enough or conscious enough or alert enough to work responsibly on a gigantic scale." Maybe not, but our imperfection runs both ways. I claim that we are not pure enough in moral character to live responsibly on a local scale, as Berry suggests; a few people in each locale, driven by greed and hubris, will attempt to exceed the bounds, and the whole process of globalization will begin afresh. It is no good to hold up the unachievable ideal of "perfect global thought" in order to promote "perfect local morals." Both ideals are impossible; reality is the messy territory in between.

─────13─────

Penetrating Prevailing Pessimism

The Case of Economic Growth and Energy

THE NEED FOR RENEWED GROWTH

Many of the worst problems faced by America today—including unemployment, the federal budget deficit, the savings and loan bailout, and low corporate profits—would be solved by steady and significant growth in the economy. If, over the next half-decade, the U.S. gross national product (GNP) were to grow at a rate of 3 to 4 percent, we would see millions of new jobs being created, we would see government tax receipts increasing (without tax rates themselves going up for each individual), we would see hundreds of billions of extra dollars becoming available to the banking system (plus a rise in real estate values), and a strong rebound in company earnings. The stock market would be justified in finding a new high, well above the Dow Jones 4,000 or 5,000.

The question of how directly to cause such growth, which was once a popular issue in Congress, has largely been abandoned by politicians—mainly, no doubt, because the treasury is empty. ("Empty" is hardly the word!) Before brilliant new

Adding Value

I have found that the best framework in which to discuss value and profit comes from the way in which physicists speak of natural processes. Left to themselves, natural processes are *entropic*. With the passage of time, they become less and less well organized. Things that are initially compact and energetic tend naturally to become widely dispersed and to lose the overall capacity for doing work. Sharp edges become dull. A freshly painted barn becomes more faded with each passing winter; eventually the roof collapses, the slats fall to the earth, the wood decays into dirt, and the "barn" no longer exists. A coiled spring naturally seeks to wind down.

As a whole, the universe itself was more highly organized when it first began than it is now. As its expansion continues, its entropy (the degree of its overall disorganization) is said to increase. The more widespread the particulate matter of the universe becomes, the less total work it is capable of doing in any one place.

In certain local regions of the universe, however, the process of entropy can be reversed, at least for a period of time—apparently for a very long period of time. The process of life, especially of human life, is properly called *anti-entropic*. By means of intelligence, humans are capable of organizing and reorganizing matter into ever more complex and powerful patterns. When this occurs, when new patterns of organization are created, and entropy is locally reversed, we may speak of *adding value* to the universe.

What actually causes profit? In my view, profit is created precisely at the moment we do something successfully that we previously did not know how to do, and when that "something" was "needed" by the universe—in the sense that entropy "needs" anti-entropy. Profit is the result of a process involving monetary capital, intellectual capital, and the creation of genuine value. Profits are taken both in money and in the knowledge of how to make further profits. Knowledge profits can often be taken from failures as well as successes.

schemes of fiscal stimulus can be tried, some sort of more "natural" economic recovery must occur, replenishing the government's ability to borrow. In the meantime, we see little from Washington beyond a verbal fracas over "protecting" ourselves from Mexico, China, and Japan.

The question of whether multiple-year, 3 to 4 percent growth (of the kind we last saw in the 1950s and 1960s) can ever occur again is debated by business economists around the country. The consensus forecast for the early 1990s is for only a weak recovery, with growth of no more than 2 percent. The position of chief executives is not to bet on stronger growth unless it actually happens. The dominant business strategy today is cost reduction, plain and simple, aimed at defending market share in a mature, slow-growth world.

FOUR CONSTRAINTS TO GROWTH

In my view, economic output will eventually boom again, but I really do not have a good guess about how far off this will be—whether years or decades. As a framework for envisioning the future, however, and as a case study in penetrating pessimism, let me suggest four main factors presently constraining economic growth, and then let me develop the last two of these in more detail. The four factors that presently constrain economic growth are: (1) complexity, (2) sustainability, (3) energy, and (4) intellectual capital.

The first factor, complexity, is an automatic product of the cumulative age of society. The longer we are around and the more of us there are, the more complex life becomes. The simple ways of adding value to the economy have already been done. Each increment of new value requires more effort, more energy, more organization, and more knowledge. Each such increment must comply with a dozen times more governmental regulations than would have been the case a generation earlier.

The second factor, sustainability, refers to our newly adopted cultural imperative, that increments of value must not merely be added to the world, but that they must be added in a way deemed to be right. New products and services must not only meet the needs of individual customers, they must also be ecologically sound. Exactly what this means is still evolving, but the new imperative is nonetheless powerful. Commercial viability is no longer assured merely by low cost and high quality, but must also meet environmental-impact requirements.

THE NEED FOR A NEW SOURCE OF CHEAP ENERGY

All four of the constraining factors are closely interrelated, but perhaps none more so than energy and intellectual capital. The surest trigger for a new economic boom would be the discovery of a new source of cheap energy. The facts of physics suggest that the potential for such a breakthrough exists (see Figure 13–1). But such a discovery simply cannot occur without a quantum leap in intellectual capital. We need genuine breakthroughs in our understanding of the physical universe, such as a solution to the problem of containing pure fusion, a method of achieving direct photoelectricity cheaply and on a grand scale, a way to build room temperature superconductors, and/or various other masterstrokes as yet unidentified.

Let us clearly distinguish these highest order demands on human knowledge from the routine energy-development activities already underway, such as the exploration and development of new oil fields and coal fields. Finding additional sources of oil, natural gas, and coal—and even converting methane, coal shale and biomass to alternative liquid fuels—I classify as "lower order" technical and commercial activities, because they are mainly price followers, not price leaders. In other words, as deposits of energy in the earth's crust dwindle, the price of energy rises and pulls in further exploration, better drilling methods,

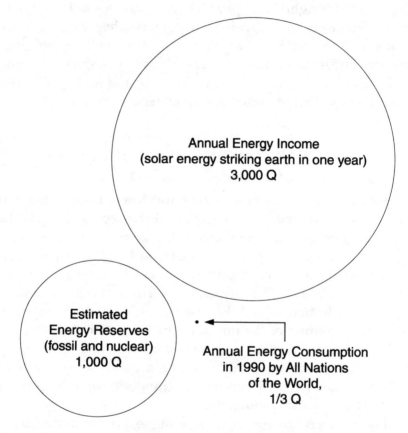

WORLD ENERGY INCOME, RESERVES, AND USE

1 "Q" = 1,000 Quadrillion BTUs ("Quads")

Annual Energy Income
(solar energy striking earth in one year)
3,000 Q

Estimated
Energy Reserves
(fossil and nuclear)
1,000 Q

Annual Energy Consumption
in 1990 by All Nations
of the World,
1/3 Q

Figure 13–1 Annual energy consumption in Year 2050, with ten billion people all of whom used same energy per capita as today's industrialized countries, would be about 3 to 5Q (• on above scale). Data from Max Singer, *Passage to a Human World*. (Reserve estimates based on work by Herman Kahn, The Hudson Institute.)

ways to convert previously unaffordable materials, and so forth. None of these lower order activities holds the potential for leap-frogging the trend of rising price, thereby producing the kind of strong economic growth previously mentioned.

As I said before, we cannot reliably predict when the higher order energy breakthroughs (fusion, photoelectricity, superconductivity, etc.) are likely to occur, nor can we even guarantee that they ever will. What we must be concerned about instead is whether we have properly set the stage. Are we maximizing the conditions under which the kind of intellectual capital needed will voluntarily accumulate?

ENERGY AND DECLINE OF COMMUNISM

In the broadest possible sense, the answer to this question is probably "yes," because in the 1990s we are witnessing the conversion of all of the world's centrally planned economies to the system of democratic capitalism. This transition is taking place in Eastern Europe, the former Soviet Union, and (more slowly at the moment) China. Political reliance on individual incentive and reward is essential to the development of scientific knowledge.

Actually, communism would probably have collapsed much earlier except for the fact of cheap energy. The case of China is a good example. China's first big oil discovery was made at Daqing in the 1950s, and the field was opened with Soviet technology in the early 1960s, before the break in relations between China and the USSR. As we know from common sense, the first helpings from a prolific resource are the easiest to obtain, and Daqing's early growth was indeed rapid—despite the political turmoil associated with Mao Tse Tung's consolidation of power. As Daqing's output rose, Mao governed the oil field with troops but successfully attributed the rise in production to the method of heroic worker brigades, so that the early bounty of the big field was transformed into a cornerstone of Chinese communist ideology. Now, however, as the productivity of the field begins to wane, and as the wastefulness of the Russians' quick-exploitation technology is seen to have dramatically reduced its overall capacity, the myth of Daqing becomes more and more apparent.

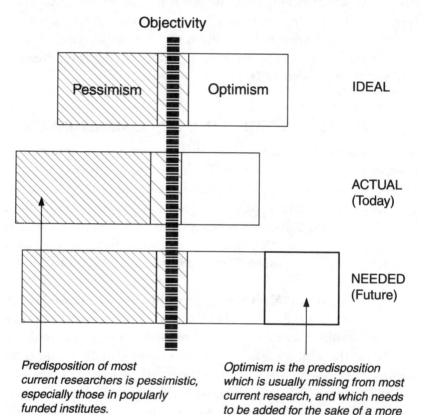

PROBLEM OF TODAY'S INDEPENDENT THINKER
If You Do Not Provide Your Own Optimism, No One Will Do It For You.

Objectivity

Pessimism | Optimism | IDEAL

ACTUAL (Today)

NEEDED (Future)

Predisposition of most current researchers is pessimistic, especially those in popularly funded institutes.

Optimism is the predisposition which is usually missing from most current research, and which needs to be added for the sake of a more objective worldview.

Figure 13–2 The source of most pessimism is the mind's lack of humility. Researchers all like to believe that their findings are accurate and complete. The process of research is inherently a setting of limits, and thus the results always seem to imply boundaries. The universe, however, is never obligated to fit within the bounds of our measurements or our reason. The universe is free to be much more complicated than we can even *imagine* it to be.

When energy is sufficiently cheap, and when it is available with "low order" technology, the inefficiency of any given political system is tolerable. But as energy becomes more expensive, a political system must enable the creation of genuine new knowledge in order to survive.

So the bootstrap of "high-order" knowledge we need to pull ahead of the trend in natural resource prices must come from the West, if it is to come at all—from America, Europe, or Japan. It makes little difference, really, in which of these three regions the knowledge accumulates, for the fruits of the discovery will be spread quickly worldwide. The whole idea that we must achieve the breakthroughs here, or lose their major benefits, is increasingly silly. There is nothing for the Japanese or the Europeans to do with new technology but to transfer it, and the same is true of the United States. Our eye must be directed at growth in the size of the entire international pie, and secondarily at our piece.

NOTHING YET AFTER FOUR DECADES OF "BIG SCIENCE"

The slowness of an energy breakthrough to emerge, however, is frankly puzzling. I would have expected one long before now. When I began my working career in 1961, at the Nuclear Weapon Laboratories in New Mexico, one of the most impressive published books I had ever seen (then or now) was a hardcover report on "Project Sherwood," the Atomic Energy Commission's investigation of pure fusion reactors. There, printed in bright two-color drawings, were all of the main technological schemes for containing high-temperature "plasmas" and harvesting the enormous energy that is unleashed when two nucleii of hydrogen unite. As I read the book, it seemed to me that unlimited energy was just around the corner—not only unlimited but, as we would say today, "clean" (or "right") in terms of the environment.

Short Term, Long Term

The movement of the universe toward greater entropy is the same movement I referred to earlier as greater diversity. In ancient times, the universe was simpler, but now it is relentlessly becoming more complex. This means that greater intellectual capital is required, in amount and in kind, to add value and gain profit. The easy work has already been done. The opportunities available in the future require more intelligence.

Monetary capital is essential to adding value, but it does not work by itself. Monetary capital, in fact, tends to be "fixed in place"; it tends to be invested in the past, in what used to work well, rather than in what will work well in the future, as the process of diversification continues. Monetary capitalists are usually "conservatives"; they oppose policies that seem to accelerate the rate of change beyond the already rapid speed that is embedded in our natural evolution; they prefer, as perhaps we all do, to earn a return without the hard work of adapting to change.

In the partnership of monetary capital and intellectual capital, the latter is invested mainly in the future, and its greatest power comes from focusing on the broad, raw problem of, "What kind of anti-entropic actions does the universe at present need?"

The reason that short-term profits are no guarantee of long-term survivability is that current earnings say nothing about how much intellectual capital the firm has, or to what future niches it has its knowledge applied. Short-term profits say nothing either about whether the firm is adding genuine value to the universe or simply "winning a game by bending its rules," as happened in the late 1980s with hundreds of U.S. savings and loans.

I was, in fact, surprised at first that the "Project Sherwood" book was unclassified, but I was told that the concepts for fusion were easy, that the trick was going to be in the execution. Later, I came to understand that the main reason for the book's existence was to convince Congress to allocate more research money, particularly for the massive particle accelerators and magnetic confinement machines envisioned by the authors. And indeed, in the 30 years since I was first introduced to the possibilities of fusion energy, all of the concepts in the book have not only been funded, but funded over and over again. And yet, after many billions of dollars of research, no sustained fusion reaction has been achieved.

In terms of "setting the stage," therefore, I wonder about our unbridled faith in "big science." I also wonder whether or not some of our potentially best scientists are "hungry" enough.

According to a story in *The New York Times* of May 28, 1991, called "Simple Device Produces Record-Breaking Cold," scientists in Boulder, Colorado were able to cool atoms of the element cesium to within one-millionth of a degree of absolute zero, which is minus 459.69 degrees Fahrenheit. At this low temperature, the metal atoms become nearly motionless, permitting the observer a close-up inspection of "what makes them tick." The record coldness was achieved with a benchtop device costing a few hundred dollars. The key to the design of the device was precision alignment and timing of six infrared lasers, shining at different directions into a vacuum chamber containing the cesium, transfixing each atom in a kind of "crossfire" of photons.

The money for the device (and for the salaries of the researchers) came jointly from the University of Colorado and from the National Institute of Standards and Technology, operated by the federal government. We cannot, therefore, criticize bigness without restraint—but the point about intellectual capital is nonetheless clear. It cannot be produced on command, or by virtue of the presence of large amounts of monetary capital, or because "lots of good minds" are working together.

✧

Competition

We may also speak of adding lesser or greater value to the universe, and, more importantly here, of adding more value to the universe than competition.

Most organisms compete with each other for the physical resources in their immediate locale, giving rise to the impression that resources themselves are limited. But the unprecedented material abundance that has been achieved in 1990s America, and in many other advanced countries, shows that "limits," if indeed they exist, lie elsewhere than in physical resources. Humans, to use the phrase of Julian Simon, are indeed "the resourceful species."

The cumulative added value produced by a group of people, in terms of material goods, moves up rapidly when the individual units are not centrally controlled but free to compete (and cooperate) with each other.

As value accumulates, it is gradually distributed further from its origin, and we can see no theoretic limit to this process. If one kind of energy becomes short, another will be substituted, given enough intellectual capital to engineer it, for the universe is fundamentally an extremely energetic arena for our affairs. Each year, about 30,000 times more solar energy strikes the surface of the earth than is used by all humans for all purposes; this solar energy is, however, dispersed; it will require more intelligence to harvest it to our uses than the forms we presently use, but it is most certainly there.

It is not possible to enumerate the thousands of exact niches that will emerge tomorrow as the best places to invest capital. One overall conclusion is clear, however: the need to reach beyond the knowledge merely of material goods. The kind of value we need most to add is breaking the view that we ourselves are of such humble resources as to perish without oil.

THE LOCUS OF GENUINE INSIGHT

There is no question that the individual mind needs other minds and that it also needs other nonintellectual resources. But when insights occur, even those that will eventually be called earth-shattering, they occur in the mind of a single individual, they do not occur "at large," say across the expanse of an entire campus or down the halls of a 5,000-person laboratory.

The most famous case of the single mind at work is no doubt Albert Einstein. What is easy to miss about the Einstein case, however, is the context in which his first big discovery took place, namely, the context for his idea about relativity. At the time when this occurred to Einstein, he was a graduate physics student, working part time in the Swiss patent office. As you would certainly guess, one of the most frequent devices under application for patent in Switzerland was the clock. As Einstein saw dozens of such applications, the stage was set for his creation of intellectual capital: No clock can keep perfect time, but only *relatively* perfect time.

The myth we have about advanced knowledge today is that it follows only and necessarily from large R&D budgets, from expensive facilities, and from making our best minds "comfortable." Not only do we give many of our big-name scientists "genius grants," it may be that we are giving them all too much money, too easily. After Einstein was comfortably housed at Princeton's Institute for Advanced Study, he produced few, if any, ideas comparable to his earlier ones.

The problem with "big science" is that the money obligates the recipients to run the little plays that the money was designated for, and not to "aim for the fence" on their own. Scientists in big projects surrender the possibility of breakthroughs in return for a continued purse. If, in the next few years, we achieve the energy breakthroughs we need for the next round of vigorous economic growth, my bet will be on the minds of the unknown "outsiders," uncomfortable, hungry, and creative.

—14—

Overcoming
General Error
The Case of Risk-Free Existence

Except in actual wartime, a politician cannot come before his or her constituents and say, "We should all be prepared to take greater risk in the future, because it is only through greater risk that we will all prosper." Something sounds wrong about this. We are not after policies that will produce more risk, but less.

Our reaction to the possibility of having to take greater risks is automatic and negative. Risk is a concept that exists in tight linkage with the idea of reduction. The phrase "reducing risk" is a basic part of our very language.

Because of its automatic connections, and because we all think we know what it means already, risk is a very difficult subject to discuss. Nonetheless, risk is a concept with enormous power to illuminate the political world we live in today and our hopes for the long-range future of that world.

In taking a fresh look at the concept of risk, let us consider several aspects of what it means, including the way our mind conceives of risk, the difference between individual risk and group risk, and the relationship between risk and prevailing conditions of material surplus rather than scarcity.

CONTRADICTION AND RISK

Two of the most remarkable capabilities of the mind are its ability to hold contradictions and its capacity for ignoring risk. The mind does not automatically reject a new principle merely because it contradicts another, earlier idea, but often finds room for both concepts to coexist in peace. Even when an unmistakable contradiction is pointed out, the offending principle may not be rejected but may sometimes become fitted even more securely in place.

Likewise, the mind does not always choose low risk over high risk. The mind is certainly capable of ranking risks, but it is also quite capable of overriding the ranking and ignoring some of the risks it knows and has quantified. The mind is especially good at ignoring small risks that are a part of the everyday routine of life.

The case of tobacco production and cigarette smoking is a frequent example of the contradictions we live with and the way in which we can ignore risks. As individuals, we know that the government simultaneously uses tax money to subsidize tobacco farming and to warn the public not to use the resulting tobacco. If we are smokers, however, we find ways to ignore the risk and continue our routine. If we are nonsmokers, we generally become bored with the repetitions of contradiction and danger and choose to ignore the whole issue.

While it seems clear that the mind does indeed quantify risks, the action is immediate and holistic and does not require such tools as pencil and paper or computer. The scale of quantification is rough. The mind can distinguish clearly, between a 10 percent risk and a 20 percent risk, if it wants to (!), but not between a 10 percent risk and an 11 percent risk. One part in ten, yes, but not one part in a hundred. And certainly not one part in a thousand or a million. (If the mind really understood one part in a million, who would play the lottery?)

---------------------- ✧ ----------------------

Knowledge and Time

"Think how efficient we would be," a partner of mine said to me recently, "if we knew what we were doing." His remark came as we reviewed the past six months of sales work and planned our calls for the first half of the next year.

The goal of compiling knowledge ahead of having to do something is easy to endorse, but difficult to execute. It is much more common to find yourself in the middle of a business effort feeling a complete lack of preparation.

The law of the universe concerning foreknowledge goes something like this: The more you know what you are doing, the less it will pay you to do it. Big money is made by doing something right that you did not know how to do before you did it. When something has been figured out, all kinds of people can do it, and the value goes down sharply.

Another way to state the same law is that if you take the time to study something thoroughly, the opportunity to do it (profitably) rapidly passes. While you are doing the study, others are involved in working out the problem. Many of the doers will fail, but some will succeed, and these will lay claim to the most profit.

So time and knowledge are inextricably linked as two parts of one continuum. The increasing of knowledge requires time, the passing of which not only deprives you of opportunities, but also presents you with a new set of crucial issues to deal with of which you have inadequate knowledge.

The competitive edge in the face of this time-knowledge duality is mainly the attitude of acceptance rather than defiance. Do not expect to achieve a lot of certainty and comfort; in fact, just the opposite, expect to be mainly uncomfortable. Abandon the investment of time in an overkill of knowledge (or "planning") that quickly and necessarily becomes obsolete.

By the way, this is not the same thing as advising you to abandon all study and planning and to jump into action with no forethought at all. Rather, the point I want to make is that going "off-line" for long, expensive research has been oversold and overemphasized; the balance needs to come decidedly back to quick experimentation in the market instead of long market research. The framework for this is the conscious recognition and acceptance of increasing diversity and uncertainty in markets and the need to apply new attitudes and styles in order to beat competition.

The mind assesses dangers quickly and avoids them if the risk is "too great." If the risk is "small," but perhaps repeated, the mind can choose to ignore it.

LANGUAGE AND RISK

The discussion of risk, however, is quite another thing, especially in the public arena. We like to pretend, in public, that our minds are perfectly logical and that we are equipped to make precise distinctions based on scientific measurements. We believe that society, unlike our own interior landscape, should be run on a system of unconflicting principles chosen for their scientific merit.

Consider the case of pesticides. Suppose we are asked, "Should society have to face a risk of ten parts in a billion of cancer from Substance A, or only one part in a billion." Our likely answer will be: "Society should opt for the small risk, not the large one."

What we have done here has nothing to do with scientific merit, but rather with the involuntary application of basic language. In listening to the question, we have heard only the "large-small" linguistic labels and reacted automatically. We have ignored the fact that we cannot, as individual human beings in everyday life, distinguish between a few parts in a billion. As stated earlier, the best we can really do is a few parts in ten. But in public discussion, we pretend that we are all data users rather than language users.

BENEFITS AND RISK

What we have also done here, by insisting always on less risk, is to ignore the fact that such reduction may cost a lot more than it is worth.

The makers of pesticides acknowledge that using their products entails a certain degree of risk. They say, however, that this small degree of risk is warranted by the large number of benefits that are obtained. They encourage people to think in terms of "benefit-to-risk" ratios, rather than in the absolute reduction of risks.

The principle that risk can be outweighed by benefits has long been a part of human culture. We might even say that the mind's capability to ignore small, routine risks is a kind of "proof" of the principle in that we all automatically accept some degree of risk for the benefit of living.

It frustrates pesticide makers today that the public will no longer accept the risks of the chemicals for their evident benefit. But however real and sensible the principle is, of thinking in terms of benefit-to-risk ratios, it is not a concept that is likely to have much impact in changing the public's mind about pesticides or other perceived hazards to the environment. The reasons for this are as follows:

1. As already mentioned, people are not professional mathematicians. People are not capable of thinking about or judging risks on the order of parts per million or parts per billion. People get the words million, billion, and trillion mixed up. If forced in public debate to make an explicit choice, people will always vote for the smallest risk and for making the smallest risk smaller. This behavior is driven by the mechanics of language, not by scientific measurement or analysis of economic consequences.

2. People in America today (rightly or wrongly) do not study the evidence around an issue, they weigh the publicity. They do not make calculations or examine the data, they listen to the media's reports of studies and its interviews of the ex-

perts. The public assumes that "truth wins out in fair debate" and that you can tell the victor by the eventual applause. No provision is made for the possibility of the debate's being involuntarily rigged.

3. The word "pesticide" is now linguistically flagged as an unusual danger to mankind. (The same is true of "ozone hole," "greenhouse effect," and "acid rain.") Today, no one needs to say, "Pesticides are dangerous," or "Pesticides are bad." The one word, pesticides, says it all, singlehandedly. Like it or not, the word has a new connotation, a bad connotation, and this feature of language far outweighs intricate calculations of economic benefits, stated in abstract units such as billions of dollars.

The prevailing opinion today is that we should pass on to future generations a world that is pesticide-free (and that has no ozone hole, no greenhouse warming, no acid rain, etc.). But if the aforementioned is right and the debate over scientific merit has been replaced by the weight of publicity and the mechanics of language, what kind of social process is this to be passing on to those same future generations?

EMOTION AND RISK

In reaction to public emotion over a number of highly publicized "food scares," the U.S. Congress is actively considering a new set of regulations for our food. The "food scares" that got Congress moving were media events. No one has actually died of Alar apples or poisoned Chilean grapes, but they could have, according to certain studies and investigations. Furthermore, say those who are the most worried, all of us face a greater risk of death than we should due to the use of chemicals such as Alar, upon which our food system has become totally dependent.

The idea now is to ban all "artificial chemicals" from food and return to foods that are completely natural, pure, and safe, and no doubt more nourishing too. Why do we have a "Pure

---⋄---

Knowledge and Money

The simplest reason for attempting to increase one's intellectual capital is its (eventual) convertability to monetary capital. The more knowledge we have, the more money we can make. Clearly, however, certain kinds of knowledge are much more profitable than others—the question is how do we determine, in advance if possible, which kinds of knowledge these are?

In one sense, the question may seem trivial, especially in an economy such as ours where the market gives its own direct answers. "They who have the greatest profits," we might be tempted to say, "are by definition those who have the greatest knowledge."

But the identity between money and knowledge is not absolute. All of us have had the experience of meeting people of great wealth who seem not to have the least amount of what we are calling knowledge; they may have inherited the money to begin with, or won it in the lottery, or in some other way have been "lucky." More frequently, they seem to have a set of abilities and attitudes that are simply "right" for what they do to earn money. People with this natural knack for profits are rarely what a college president would call "well-educated," and when asked, "How do you do it?" are not able to say anything that allows us to imitate them or that strikes us as "knowledgeable." I am not talking here about the person who knows how to do something fairly simple but who has chosen to do it at the *right time* and made big profits, for I would surely include timing as a branch of knowledge—unless, of course, the person in question really had no choice about when to do it and was lucky.

Another kind of knowledge that undoubtedly makes money is the branch that deals with "rules of the game." Lawyers, bankers, brokers, and many other kinds of businesspeople add a great deal of value to our economy by developing, refining, interpreting, organizing, testing, pushing, and even breaking the rules. My own abilities and preferences, however, do not lie in this direction, and to be faithful to my own precepts I must spend more time talking about the kinds of knowledge that add value to products and services than about the kinds that, however indispensable, merely help us achieve better rules and swifter execution.

Another kind of person we have all no doubt met, in contrast to those of wealth already mentioned, is the person who has seemingly great knowledge but who has no great amount of monetary wealth. Professors of literature, philosophy, history, art, education, and various other "nonscientific" or "nonbusiness" disciplines seem often to occupy this category, especially the more interested they are in elaborate, academic theory as opposed to small pieces of practical knowledge that work in the marketplace.

Lastly, in this list of flaws in the connection between intellectual capital and monetary capital, is the person who is either extraordinarily clever but not genuinely knowledgeable, or who has knowledge well ahead of his or her time. The example comes to mind here of Buckminster Fuller, who was certainly knowledgeable in engineering science, and who though not a pauper was likewise never able to communicate his vaster ideas and visions beyond a very small, dedicated group.

Food and Drug Act" (from the 1920s) if not for this very purpose? Something must have gone wrong in the meantime for all of these chemicals to have crept in. It was probably that old defect of American culture, excess profits.

Contradictions in the idea of ridding our food supply of all artificial chemicals appear immediately, which ought to be quite powerful and persuading. What exactly is an "artificial chemical" versus a "natural chemical"? Is not everything a chemical? Does natural food have no chemicals? In fact, doesn't natural food have so many harmful "natural chemicals" that we have sought with great determination to overpower them with other chemicals for our own safety? And has this not worked? Has our lifespan not increased substantially over the past several decades? And at the same time, has our food supply not become more secure, less expensive, and altogether more varied, better tasting, and more nutritious? Should we not have been willing to pay someone for this? Do we have any evidence that we have paid in excess and that our farmers and our food companies have been prospering unfairly? (Hardly! Farm income today must be supported by the government to make it comparable to urban income, and food company profits have been so low for so long that restructuring has taken place throughout the industry.)

LEGISLATION AND RISK

Pointing out these logical contradictions, of course, has had very little impact. The push is on for new and tighter regulations that will make our food safe again.

In fact, the largest of all the contradictions in this event is that despite the jokes about there already being too many lawyers and too many bureaucrats, and despite the professed desire for more "nature" in our lives, the impact of new food regulations will be just the opposite: more litigation, more bureaucracy, and more technology. The new regulations, if they are to be "tighter," will have to be more intricate and will have to rely on ever more precise technical measurements of the offending chemicals. This will provide a picnic for lawyers, bureaucrats, and scientists, complete with their own special language: "hazard identification," "dose-response assessment," "exposure assessment," "risk characterization," and so on. These are a puzzle for the rest of us.

The new food regulations, then, will be another in the pile up of American legislative snafus, which we will later acknowledge as contributing to the decline of our international competitiveness. The new food regulations will be designed by scientific experts, modified and codified by scientific amateurs (Congresspeople and their young aides), and applauded by the public (which has been driven mainly by media events rather than intelligent consideration). The regulations will lead to more litigation, more technology, and perhaps to worse food at higher costs. If the risk of death is lessened (will we eventually make it simply illegal to die?), it will be by a miniscule degree.

To oppose further regulation is completely unfashionable. To oppose the reduction of risk is to encounter a maelstrom of rhetoric perfected in recent years by so-called "public interest groups." The rhetoric goes as follows:

> How can you oppose reducing the risk of death? How can you argue that any economic benefit to farmers, food companies, and the country is worth risking the life of a single child? How can you argue that our children and our children's children should not have apples that are completely safe? How can you ask some people, involuntarily, to assume greater risk so that others (for instance, a few thousand greedy apple farmers) can profit?

MATERIAL SUCCESS AND RISK

Each element of the preceding rhetoric fails, of course, under the light of reason. But the majority of Americans are not listening to it with intelligent skepticism.

The rhetoric has become especially powerful at the present juncture in our history. It fills a void in the American psyche while we search for the next valid mission of our culture. The mission void has been created not by the failure of our culture, but indeed by its extraordinary success. We have been so successful in the production of material goods, perhaps especially food, that we now have the luxury of subjecting ourselves to rhetorical self-flagellation, . . . avoiding momentarily an answer to the question, "What do we do next?"

Our dominant cultural imperative since the beginning of recorded history has been to succeed materialistically: to have enough food, to have clothes and shelter, to have health care, and so on. This we have done in America to a degree unprecedented in human history. All other nations of the world are attempting to emulate us. Yet we cannot quite see the juncture for what it is, as success rather than failure. We have not yet accepted the larger question, let alone found a good answer. "What do we do next, having achieved material success beyond belief?" Fault the way we did it? Assume that it cannot last? Save the earth from our folly? Reduce risk to zero?

THE FUTURE AND RISK

The risks that have been most productive to society have been the risks taken by individuals. It is individual risk-taking that matters the most to our future. Individuals, one by one, mentally calculate the risk of given actions and make their decisions accordingly. Individuals who calculate accurately and execute successfully are said to produce profit. The higher the risk that is overcome, the greater the profit. In an important sense, profit is defined as that which follows the overcoming of risk, and thus the concept of risk is seen to be even more intimately woven into the concept of democratic capitalism than we can fully appreciate.

In any particular group of people, there will be relatively few who will take high-risk actions that produce profit, and many more who will take only low-risk actions. The function of government, in any such group, is always to reduce the overall riskiness of conditions, in conformance with the desire of the majority. The government attempts to perform this mandate, of reducing risk, by passing laws and regulations.

There is little point in complaining about the basic process, even about the inevitable complexity and turgidness added to the system by government. What we should object to is attempts by the government, or by those who are influencing it, to reduce risk to zero and to reduce risk without reference to our competitiveness with other nations. Both of these directions represent

142

fundamental misunderstandings of how the universe works. To seek zero risk is to seek immortality, which is simply to deny reality. To regulate so intensively that we stymie our individual entrepreneurs more than those of our competitor countries is to worsen the prospects for our future and the world's future, rather than to protect it.

Perhaps the largest objection to greater constraint of risk-taking by our society is the fact of its being driven by emotion rather than by the light of reason. Suppose for the moment that the dubious proposition of environmentalists were true, that the earth itself is imperiled by humankind's very presence. What we would then most want to pass on to future generations is an honest ability to assess facts, size up the risks, and take profitable action. What we least want to pass on is a mythical concept of being able to preserve our "natural" environment, risk-free.

The remainder of this book deals with two main kinds of exercises for increasing intellectual capital.

New Approaches for the Individual

The essential element is attitude. An individual facing risk, for instance, is better served by real knowledge than by credentials recommended by others. An individual facing risk will want to rely mainly on his or her right hand and not on the left. An individual stands a much better chance of adding real value to the universe by relying on his or her core abilities than on secondary strengths, or on training he or she may have pursued to conform to the cultural myth of "business administration." To the degree that individuals do rely on "core abilities" to add value, they will say that they are "doing what they like best," and their level of stress will be greatly reduced.

New Approaches for the Company

The key here is also attitude. A company or other large organization facing risk tends almost automatically to heighten the

---✧---

Stress

The relationship between knowledge and profit defies perfect planning. It is much more a simultaneous connection than a sequential one. An infinite build-up of knowledge does not guarantee an infinite profit, because of competition and because the universe is moving toward complexity much faster than we can learn about it. So in my view, profit is created at the precise moment we do something successfully that we previously were not sure how to do. (Or when we do something we already know how to do at a *time* that turns out to be the "right time" or the "opportune time.")

If this view is correct, then profit and stress are intimately related, because of the inherent risk of failure involved in every attempt to add value. The idea of business without stress is as nonsensical as the notion of profits without risk. The possession of intellectual capital can *lower* risk, but never eliminate it. There are no sure ways of adding value to the universe.

---

inherent stress by means of (1) employing elaborate preplanning processes that will supposedly lead to "success without failure," and (2) shunning honest and open criticism of the high failure rate that it inevitably incurs.

In all cases, the key element to enhanced intellectual capital—and thus to added value, profit, and stress reduction—is adoption of attitudes that conform more to reality than to myth. The basic principle is certainly easy, but not its execution.

— ✧ —

PART THREE

Positive Approaches and Techniques

——15——

Everyday Habits at the Office

FINDING AND KEEPING THE TOUGHEST "KERNELS"

Competent managers know that in every business initiative there is some kernel that is theirs alone to know about and to decide upon. This kernel will be the toughest part of the overall situation and it will be associated with the least certainty, the least good information, but the most risk.

An example might be the choosing of a name for a new product. Many candidates will be suggested; however, the final choice of a name belongs to the product manager. This is his or her business kernel and cannot be delegated. The right name pulls together all dimensions of marketing—promotion, price, product, and distribution—and makes them work together.

Cracking the kernel is the way a manager progresses up the scale of competence, let's say from a level of "7" to a level of "8." Kernels lie at the extreme leading edge of one's business knowledge; the "right answer" to a kernel question cannot be known without trial and error. But it is helpful to recognize ahead of time that this is true; it is helpful to remember that you will come up against these kernels, from time to time, and that you cannot assign them to someone else. They are a focus for your courage and a prime place to apply your intellectual honesty.

MAKING "ROOM ON THE PLATE"

The CEO of my company once told me that he saw his workload like the food on a plate. When you take on too much, your plate is too full. You become anxious to finish everything, and you push yourself faster and faster to finish. And then along comes someone with another helping, whether you want it or not, and it looks as delicious as the rest.

How you choose to handle this condition is crucial both to you and to the company. How do you manage your workload to get the maximum done, without the paralysis of overload?

I recommend the following two rules: (1) You must always have part of your plate empty (i.e., you must always maintain some reserve capacity); and (2) you must accept full responsibility for selecting what must be dumped to create the reserve.

When your plate is overflowing, you will look at your calendar and you see that every moment is preplanned. You will feel controlled by events. You will feel "programmed." Your to-do list will go on forever. There will never be a time in which you are free for something genuinely new and spontaneous, or for when you (and you alone) must handle one of the "kernels" mentioned above. In this situation, you will never feel fresh, but behind, buried, and guilty. This does not work. Part of your plate must always be empty.

In any list of tasks, all will be deserving, but not all will be equal. The lesser ones must be ruthlessly cut. It is far better to accept responsibility for making a cut and cutting the wrong thing, than to make no cuts at all and stagger along under the false belief that one day you will make it to a natural clearing. In business, all clearings are created; you have to make them yourself. You are better off to gamble that you are making a clearing of the right trees than not ever to make a clearing.

To put it another way, doing every job on your list poorly will probably mean that your boss gives you a poor rating. Doing only the "right" jobs on your list well will probably mean that your boss gives you a good rating. Cutting the "right" jobs from your list and not doing them at all might mean a poor rating, but it might also mean that your boss has a chance to help you improve your judgment rather than downgrade your actual performance.

Managing your workload by "ruthlessly cutting the least deserving jobs" gives you room on your plate for a daily helping of "new top priorities," and forces you and your boss to get your real priorities straight.

Delegating to Create Wealth

Whenever I feel unusually swamped, there are two kinds of things I wonder about:

- What items can be ruthlessly cut from my list to make room for others?

- What items can be *delegated* to someone else?

My tendency has always been not to delegate enough, in the fond belief that only I can do it right and in the fear that failure must be avoided at all costs.

To be an effective manager requires skill in delegating—neither too much nor too little, neither too soon nor too late. Can a fail safe system be developed for this process? I doubt it, but I think several important distinctions can be made.

First of all, it is easy to delegate things that do not matter; it is hard to delegate things that do. If it does not matter whether your agent succeeds or fails, then there is nothing in it for him or her, or for you. Your own reach will not be extended. Unless your agent's failure would actually be hurtful, then neither of you can gain from the act of delegation.

Second, it makes sense to try small items before large and to proceed along a path of growth that emphasizes clear, two-way communication.

Third, the qualities you must seek in an agent are the following: (1) common sense, (2) the combination of humility and confidence, and (3) a sincere interest in teamwork.

Fourth, at the far end of the spectrum, there are items that you cannot delegate, even if you are a chief executive. There will be in every business situation, if you are doing your job right, a kernel of thought-action that only you can perform. This kernel will always be at the frontier, it will require outright courage, and there will never be sufficient data or analysis to relieve you of having to gamble your entire stake. This is what you are paid to do, and this is why business cannot be automated.

When you delegate properly, what happens is the birth of organizational wealth. If you have chosen the right agent and the right task, then the agent steps out into a richer flow of information than before, and he or she has the potential to handle it with more global concepts. If concepts are formed that work, then the agent gets "smarter" and so does the whole organization.

ACTING WITHOUT PERFECT LOGIC

Once in a great while I am completely logical, I decide the merits of a course of action, to the best of my ability, on the basis of facts and the relative probabilities of different outcomes, benefits, and penalties.

In public, all of us pretend that we are perfectly rational. No one disagrees that logic should be supreme. From the standpoint of business, however, the cultural wish for more rationality supports three important fallacies that the independent business mind should try to break.

1. *The fallacy of complete information.* This is a great favorite of scientists. "If we only had more data," they say, "we could make better decisions." There are two problems with what the scientists urge: (1) We are already absolutely awash in data and cannot interpret what we have, and (2) it is simply never possible to gather the *right* data on the things that truly matter, because these things always have to do with human motives anyway.

2. *The fallacy of causal clarity.* This is the favorite of lawyers. In this fallacy, it is assumed that every event can be precisely described in terms of its essential causes. The trouble again is that the key events are always human ones, and our motives are always a mixture of ill-defined emotions. Anyone who has ever worked for a large corporation knows that it is simply never clear why a company does something, or not; the choice of corporate initiatives has to do more with who has the most charm in the boardroom than with the outright merits of the opportunities.

3. *The fallacy of profit without risk.* This is also known as the bureaucratic fallacy, and it follows closely from the two previous errors of believing that we can obtain complete information and of believing that we can exactly know all the causes. It is certainly trite to say that there is no profit without risk; but it is not possible to exaggerate the direct connection between profit and risk. I claim that "profit" is exactly that which results when something is done right for which there was inadequate foreknowledge of how it should be done. Risk and profit are not just closely related, they are virtually synonymous.

The independent business thinker will not, of course, abandon reason, because of the aforementioned fallacies. Instead, in any given profit opportunity, he or she will seek *sufficient* data, an *adequate* grasp of the causes, and the courage to risk making a mistake, in the course of which he or she will either add value to the world or be better prepared to do so the next time.

LAUGHING MORE AT MISTAKES

One of the many sources of stress in business life is the apparent need to do the impossible. A good example is predicting the future. The seriousness with which we attempt the impossible, day after day, is amazing.

"But how else," you say, "can wise investment decisions be made? If I don't foresee conditions accurately, I'll fail."

A better approach to this situation is to recognize that while you cannot predict the future, you might just possibly be able to predict it better than your competitors. If you can do so, even by a tiny margin, you will have a leg up on survival, and perhaps even on prosperity.

Let's say you make this recognition, and now, rather than wanting to forecast the future with absolute perfection, you want to do it marginally better than the competition. How should you proceed? What other new attitudes will help?

The first thing I recommend is to discourage seriousness and to encourage levity. Yes, I think you should try to increase your laughter.

The reason is simple. If you have recognized that you cannot do the impossible, at least not perfectly (but maybe better than a few others), then the next step is openly to acknowledge your errors. You have always made lots of errors, and you always will. But aren't they easier to take and to learn from if you are laughing and if your colleagues are laughing too?

Laughter relieves stress, as we all know. People say, "Nothing feels better than a good laugh." Then why not do it more? Why not adopt it as a strategy to improve your business performance?

The answer here is obvious: It is not customary. Business is a serious business. You cannot go around laughing at things that may cause millions of dollars to be lost, and perhaps uprooting the lives of thousands of people. It is simply not appropriate.

A determination to be serious in appraising and forecasting business conditions has no better odds of beating competition than any other approach. The annals of American business are littered with hundreds of serious, analytical methods that were supposed to work, but didn't. Has "coldly rational strategic planning" done the trick for American business?

I think the answer is plainly no. And yet the convention remains to keep trying the impossible. The goal is still to apply perfect rationality to business.

By definition, rationality is pure logic without interference from emotionality. The joke is simply that humans are put on earth with a dual nature, a two-sidedness. One part of the brain sees things logically; another part sees things in terms of feelings. This other part does not proceed from point to point; it grasps wholes without being told to; it sees odd patterns without instructions; it permits tears when they are not wanted.

What the logical part of the brain sees may be in simultaneous contradiction with what the emotional part sees. At the moment in time when consciousness apprehends the contradiction, the physiological response is (by definition) laughter.

Years of practiced seriousness can cause us to suppress our laughter. This in turn allows us to deny that any contradictions exist, as between logic and feeling, or between fact and fancy. A further general result for business is the decrease in our capacity to learn from our mistakes. Criticism is simply too hard to take when the audience is deadly serious. So emerges business "doubletalk," that famous style of jargon used to deny contradictions that are obvious to everyone but can't be mentioned.

If millions of dollars and thousands of lives really are at stake, is it not important to try unusual—even unconventional—approaches? If levity helps the human mind to learn from errors and perhaps to forecast the future better, wouldn't we all benefit from changing the iron rule of seriousness?

The answer is yes, but the change would be very difficult. The change is not one of mere technique; it is not a matter of everyone bringing a joke book to the next staff meeting. The change, for most businesspeople, is revolutionary; what is required is that we see ourselves not as leading actors in a Shakespearian tragedy, but rather as bit players in a global comedy. This demands more humility than most of us can muster.

"Wow," a friend of mine says about this concept, "you can't mean it! They'll never take you seriously."

I have no doubt that my suggestion will not be taken seriously. If anything gets laughed at, it will be the approach just described. To conclude, there are three points of defense for the aforementioned.

1. A comedy is not the same thing as a joke. I do not think that life, or business, is a joke. But neither do I think it must be treated as a monumental tragedy. Seeing life more as a comedy than as a tragedy may permit us to acknowledge errors better than our competition and to make marginally better forecasts.

2. Customers are no more fully rational than we are. The key to serving the customer better, which should drive every business, is to stop treating him or her as a statistical abstraction that carefully reasons every purchase.

3. In business, if it works, it needs no defense. Try it! If the degree of seriousness declines from 9.5 to 9.4 on a scale of 10, the resulting increment of cheerfulness will be worth it.

16

Qualities to Seek and Enlarge

INTELLECTUAL HONESTY

In American culture, "honesty" is usually defined as the "absence of dishonesty." An honest person is one who does not lie, cheat, steal, or take unfair advantage. By this traditional definition, most readers of this book are no doubt completely honest.

But the normal way to judge dishonesty, and thus its opposite, is by overt behavior. Suppose, however, that I never see you steal, nor does anyone else. Does that prove you are honest? Especially, does that prove you have "intellectual honesty"? In other words, how do we define honesty in a positive sense when no external behavior is involved or when the behavior is not something covered by the canon of law? What happens when you are merely giving a recommendation on some business decision, based perhaps on your research, or based on no more than your own experience? How do I know that you are reporting the research faithfully? How do I know that you have checked the facts rigorously? How do I know you are not already convinced of the rightness of one course over another, especially if you stand to gain personally? How do I know, in other words, if you have "intellectual honesty"?

I assert that most readers are not dishonest in the usual sense, they are not thieves, but most readers of this book cannot go through the preceding list of descriptors of intellectual honesty without having a few twinges of conscience.

My experience in business is that this is the area of greatest potential for being smarter than the competition, that is, to be more honest, to have more intellectual honesty, and to unlock and enable the creation of more intellectual capital.

Business decisions are often made during high emotion. This is a given. But the habit of intellectual honesty, accompanied by the courage to use it and to speak out for its results, will bring the individual and the firm a greater competitive advantage. Most businesses and most teams of executives prefer not to face reality; they prefer to see things the way they *want* them to be rather than the way they are. Since reality always wins in the end, the edge is there for those who want to face reality early and squarely.

Enhancing your singular stock of intellectual capital requires the cultivation, more than anything else, of a quality called "intellectual honesty." The concept of intellectual honesty defies easy formulation. What I have tried to do is to list a large number of overlapping aspects of honesty, like suspending a diamond by a thread and letting it turn in the sun. The reader should proceed through the entire list slowly and then come back to the entrees that fit him or her best.

Descriptors of Intellectual Honesty

- Being able to say, and saying, what you really believe rather than repeating the views of others.

- Being comfortable with the phrase, "I don't know."

- Being able to accept evidence that changes your mind, especially when your most precious views are involved.

- Being able to talk in plain, clear language, especially about your own motives.

- Preferring simple relationships instead of complex ones.

- While preferring simplicity, being able to judge when complexity fits an emerging situation better.

- Being able to "print out" your net position and to argue for it forcefully, in the hopes that another person with superior reason will find its flaws.

- Seeking criticism from the most powerful sources whenever convenient rather than avoiding such people until your position is "better prepared."

- Finding as much value in unanswered questions as in so-called complete answers.

- Having confidence through humility rather than the majesty of your organizational position.

- Knowing when details must be mastered before general conclusions can be trusted.

- Understanding that powerful concepts may illuminate much, yet simultaneously hide even more.

- Having private irreverence for the values of one's culture, while in no way abandoning them, and having skepticism without cynicism.

- Being able to make careful separation between point-to-point logic (discursive thought) and analogy (metaphor).

- Being able to separate the *understanding* of a (business) situation from the *selling* of a solution.

- Knowing that form is equal in power to substance and that a good presentation can sell a bad finding.

- Being able to swim longer than others in chaos before seizing on an order, but not too long.

The three most troublesome aspects of intellectual honesty for me have been: (1) being able to accept evidence that changes your mind, especially when your most precious views are involved, (2) seeking criticism from the most powerful sources available rather than avoiding such people until "later," and (3) understanding that powerful concepts may illuminate much, yet simultaneously hide even more.

HUMILITY

Business is the home of experts. Our insistence that someone else *must* know something that we do not, that someone must, in fact, know something that is essentially unknowable, borders on the absurd. Instead of this attitude that we can "buy knowledge from experts," I recommend the cultivation of genuine humility in the face of our enormous ignorance, as human beings, of the vast universe around us.

The provinces of our knowledge can be divided as shown in Figure 16–1. The provinces are

1. What we know,

2. What we know we don't know, and

3. What we don't know we don't know.

Strictly speaking, Province 3, which is ignorance, could be represented by a circle of infinite size. The world is not only more complicated than we think it is, it is more complicated than we can imagine it to be. But the circle as shown in Figure 16–1 is large enough for illustration; we must respect our ignorance but not be paralyzed by it.

There is another cause for humility in Figure 16–1 besides the proportionate scale of our ignorance. Category 1 can be subdivided as follows:

1. What we know, some of which:

   a. We know we know,

   b. We don't know we know,

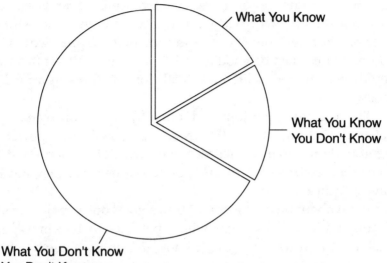

Figure 16–1 Market knowledge.

c. We think we know but don't, and

d. We know but don't have enough confidence to argue for.

ADMITTING, "I DON'T KNOW"

When the president of the United States faces a press conference, it is nearly impossible for him to say, "I don't know," even though many of the questions have been designed to draw him off base. How frequently do we hear a national leader say, "I don't know, I'll check on it and get back to you"? The essence of leading is apparently to have answers ahead of the followers. We want to believe that a leader is bigger than life, with comprehension that towers above normal, in any of a thousand subject matters that might arise. We would prefer leaders to be more God-like than human. In the Age of Television, of course, the exact same audience for a press conference is never assembled twice, so getting *back* with further information is not strictly possible. Furthermore, it can be argued that the president of the United States *must* be good at quick answers, because the issue could be a matter of life and death for us all, as in a nuclear attack.

But in demanding to be led, often by "quick answers," and never permitting "I don't knows," we forsake the power of rigorous honesty. In its absence, we turn right around and lament the "dishonesty" of our politicians because they always have a "quick answer."

What about businesspeople? Can a good business leader say, "I don't know"? Can anyone who expects to advance in wage or position afford to say, "I don't know"? Don't we rise by being the one with the right answers at the right time?

In business, we are not on television. Audiences can always be reassembled. We are not in command of the military. What we want is better decisions than our competitors, which means both accuracy and timeliness. Accuracy goes hand in hand with honesty, especially in the sense of dismissing any ego that will skip over missing facts in pursuit of personal recognition. The fundamental attitude needed to comprehend markets better than competitors is humility.

Timeliness is not unimportant, but it is secondary. *People never remember how fast you do something, only how well.*

Next time a question puts you on the spot, try the honest way out: "I don't know, but I'll check on it and get back to you." Then, of course, do it, and do it well.

GIVING AND TAKING CRITICISM

Of all the things in which "give" and "take" are partners, criticism is perhaps the most important. It is this partnership that recognizes that life, especially in business, is a long series of opportunities to improve your batting average. Some averages are high, some are low, but none are a perfect 1.000, or even close.

A company in which no one is afraid to make a mistake is rare. A company in which people are frightened to death of making a mistake is common.

There are few managers in any company, of course, who would not agree that we all must learn by "trial and error," but this is lip service. What is normally meant today by corporate trial and error is "successful trial with no error."

We all know that the purpose of business is to succeed, not to fail. What we forget is this: *Success cannot be defined without intimate knowledge of failure.* To define what something is, you need to know lots about what it isn't. This is sometimes called "contributing to *The Journal of Negative Results*." In the aftermath of any such contribution, however, we are most likely to be in lots of pain: *Nothing hurts worse than being wrong except when everyone knows.* Since it is not possible never to make mistakes, we must ask ourselves, "Can anything be done to ease the pain, but enable the gain?"

My recommendations are shown in Figures 16–2 and 16–3, which are meant as *partners.* "Giving" is no good unless you are good at "taking." Giving without taking ignores the inevitable: If you are in the right today, you will be in the wrong tomorrow. If not, you are not taking enough risk to make your firm competitive. And thus, for being too conservative, you are in the wrong.

Being the boss should do nothing to the partnership of give and take. Being the boss does not give you the option of giving but not taking, and it certainly does not give you a license for fault-finding, blame, and condemnation, unless you want those you supervise frozen with fear and riling with resentment.

Joining the partnership of give and take can be done from either direction. If you want to learn how to take, learn how to give, or vice versa.

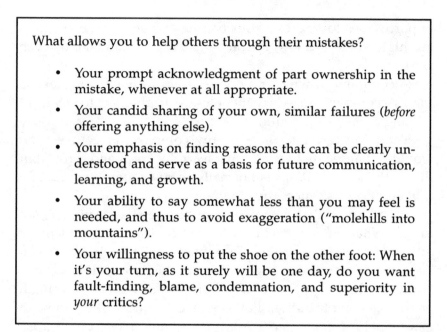

What allows you to help others through their mistakes?

- Your prompt acknowledgment of part ownership in the mistake, whenever at all appropriate.

- Your candid sharing of your own, similar failures (*before* offering anything else).

- Your emphasis on finding reasons that can be clearly understood and serve as a basis for future communication, learning, and growth.

- Your ability to say somewhat less than you may feel is needed, and thus to avoid exaggeration ("molehills into mountains").

- Your willingness to put the shoe on the other foot: When it's your turn, as it surely will be one day, do you want fault-finding, blame, condemnation, and superiority in *your* critics?

Figure 16–2 Giving criticism.

ENTHUSIASM

Fifteen years ago I was working on a project to make human food protein directly from soybeans. To me, the project was meant to save the world from hunger. I worked on it night and day. Somewhat by luck, I found a scientist who had a new technology for separating the bean's protein from its other materials, while at the same time eliminating the bad taste we all associate with soy. "This is it!" I said to myself, "a product that will make us millions!"

I scheduled an emergency meeting with my boss to tell him my news and to get money to proceed. But before I had finished the story, he stopped me, looked me directly in the eye, and said, "Your enthusiasm isn't selling me."

I have never been the same since. This was the time in my life when I learned, at the deepest level, that the crucial currency

---

What allows others to help you through your mistakes?

- Your frank acknowledgment of responsibility (instead of denial).
- Your ability to state what has happened in plain language (instead of euphemism and excuse).
- Your desire to understand the *reasons* for failure, to accept them, to learn, and to try again.
- Your willingness to listen to suggestions for alternative approaches in the future.

Figure 16–3 Taking criticism.

of business is reason, not emotion. My basic enthusiasm for business and for life in general remains undiminished. But now what I am most enthusiastic about is finding rational strategies that will beat the competition and letting facts enroll a larger team to do the fighting.

What, then, is a PRODUCT CHAMPION, if not the Captain of Enthusiasm? Clearly, a product champion must have enthusiasm. His or her enthusiasm hooks the interest of others, but it does not land the catch. You cannot fish without it, but you cannot live from the bait alone.

Can enthusiasm coexist with patience? Let us say first that when the two do *not* coexist, an *independent* entrepreneur is born. When a product champion is impatient, and not open to suggestions from others, he or she often leaves the parent organization. His or her enthusiasm, by itself, has not sold.

A partnership between a large company and an entrepreneur can occur, however, when they both make allowances for the sublimely human nature of enthusiasm. The company must see it as a precious commodity, to be nurtured. The individual champion must see it in himself or herself for what it is, emotion, and make a new commitment to reason.

Personal enthusiasm that motivates rational inquiry, proof by trial and error, and the enrollment of teams is a winner for all concerned.

CREATIVITY

New and better ideas are a part of human culture. In any group of people of significant size that has come together for any common activity, new and better ideas will be generated automatically, whether you want them or not.

The role of human life in the universe, insofar as it can presently be seen, is to change it with new ideas. If "entropy" is the name for the steady degradation of energy toward an ultimate temperature of absolute zero, then human life is *anti-entropic;* intelligence, of itself, spontaneously generates heat. Ideas create more and greater organization, rather than letting things run down.

If this is true, if bright ideas are "normal," why is it so hard, in business, to get a new idea approved? The answer to this question revolves around three further observations about ideas, people, and companies:

1. Ideas do not occur to everyone in a group at once. Committees do not have ideas. Ideas occur to a single human mind.

2. The person with a new idea must therefore communicate it to others. He or she may not be good or forceful at communicating and may not feel welcome to do so.

3. The business environment generally favors conformity ahead of creativity. The best "idea" person in a company (except perhaps the founder) will have proven himself or herself as a team player, first, before he or she has been able to produce new ideas that are welcome, and that therefore work. The best idea person will know what is meant by *bootstrapping,* the ability to do one job, as it is, while simultaneously birthing another.

The degree to which new ideas are "creative" is shown in Figure 16–4. To be creative, an idea must be far enough away from the existing body of thought and action, but not *too* far. Ideas that are too far removed are perceived as "far out."

All new ideas, when they are first generated and communicated, have a way of seeming "further out" than they are. It is the job of the creators to scout the frontier, but not lose sight of the wagon train. If they do, they are on their own.

The job of the manager is to create an environment in which the business can be run from day to day, but in which new ideas

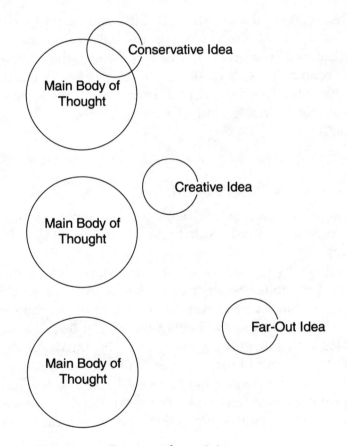

Figure 16–4 Degrees of creativity.

are welcome and can be heard. The job of the manager is further to select among the forthcoming ideas those that are far enough out, but not too far, to be capable of team execution, and to explain to staff and management what the connection is to the main body of thought and action.

In the recent book, *Breakthroughs!*, two vice presidents of the Arthur D. Little consulting company, P. R. Nayak and J. M. Kettringham, acknowledge that new ideas originate in all types of settings, but usually tumble out onto rocky soil. "All too often, when creativity is gaining momentum, upper management feels compelled to swoop down and 'take charge'." The ideal breakthrough manager, in the Arthur D. Little study, was a certain Italo Trapasso, a top executive with the Italian chemical giant, Montedison; when he was assigned to manage the company's research center, Trapasso treated his researchers with more reverence than his superiors. "All I did was to recognize the merit of the people. I was a kind of servant to them. I was their assistant."

OPTIMISM

Optimism is the quality that sends a businessperson back for more in the face of markets that reject 95 out of every 100 new initiatives.

In philosophy, the theory of optimism consists of reasons for why good preponderates over evil. The theory of pessimism is the opposite, consisting of reasons for why evil preponderates over good. As we all know, neither theory can be proven with airtight logic. Businesspeople rarely enter this philosophical debate. What matters in business is to *be* optimistic, not to argue about it. What matters in business is for leaders to see, in each failure, the germ of a new way to succeed. What matters is for the whole team to enroll with full enthusiasm in each new attempt.

An old joke in research circles goes: "What's the difference between an optimist and a pessimist?" Answer: "The pessimist is the one with the facts."

The joke confirms that most research, especially *market* research, and more especially market research with vast amounts of economic and demographic data, is much more suited to "shooting down" ideas than to launching new ones. Research provides more help to perfectionists than to imperfectionists.

Objectivity, to the extent that it can be achieved, requires us to provide our own optimism. If you do not provide the optimism, no one will do it for you, because we live in a world of pervasive pessimism.

The fundamental necessity of optimism in business discourages criticism, skepticism, irreverence, and other qualities that seem negative. But as competence builds, the mature business leader gains interest in building intellectual capital by all the diverse ways possible. Only among his or her peers and close colleagues, however, can he or she be fully critical, and even in this circle with caution. No matter what high praise we give to complete reason and objectivity, the essential quality of a business leader is to provide optimism and to see the cup with precisely 50 percent water in it as "half full."

17

Techniques of Selecting Information and Building Knowledge

IS READING WORK?

One morning I got to work early and began reading *The New York Times*. There were some interesting items on that particular day, so I leaned back in my chair, put my feet up on my desk, and became oblivious to all else—the newspaper blocking my view. Shortly there came a tap at my office door and the company's chief executive said, "Good morning! You got a minute?"

Hastily I took my feet from my desk and put down the newspaper. The clock said 8:15 A.M. The question was, had the boss caught me on company time not working, or had the boss interrupted the most important work of my day?

My initial response was that I had been doing something I should not have been, that once the work day has begun I should concentrate on memos, telephone calls, and decision making, and put aside something so frivolous as the newspaper.

The first response in this case—developed from cultural conditioning before profits became so directly dependent on constantly expanding knowledge—is wrong. Survey after survey in recent years has confirmed that today's businessperson gets most of his or her market knowledge from reading, and specifically from reading the newspaper, *not* from watching television.

Far from cutting short his or her reading, the job of the successful knowledge worker is to *read better than his or her competition.* Two keys to better reading are attitude and technique.

The best attitude is to fight the old feeling that reading the paper is wasting time. Properly reading the paper is work. The job is beating the competition with better knowledge.

The best technique is not speed reading, but something called *active passivity.* Picture your mind in a calm attitude. Picture your mind like a still pool of water into which the items from the paper will fall like pebbles. In this metaphor, the quality of your understanding is equivalent to how strong and clear are the ripples. The calmer the pool, the more distinct the ripples, the further they can reach, and the broader is your understanding. To achieve the best results in reading, to gather genuinely new insights and break wrong opinions, you must *actively* make your mind *passive.* This takes practice, but even more importantly, it takes the attitude that what you are doing is work.

COMPETITIVE READING I

It is reported that about 50,000 books are published every year in the United States, which would be about 1,000 per week. Of these, roughly half are nonfiction, so there would be about 500 nonfiction titles per week, or almost 100 per working day.

If you purchased these 100 books and merely flipped through them, almost as you would rifle a deck of cards at its edge, spending no longer than a single second on ten pages, it would take you half an hour. And unless your reading speed was 250,000 words per minute, instead of the normal 250, you would get little from your effort.

There is no point then in worrying about reading *everything*. It would require you to be 1,000 times smarter than everyone else. It really is not possible. Yet many ambitious executives feel vaguely guilty that they "don't keep up."

It is also reported that one out of every four college graduates reads one book a year. If this is true, and my own acquaintances seem to bear this figure out, then a way opens up out of the guilt: I call it *competitive reading*. What I mean is simply reading more than your competitors, reading the best books (for you), and *reading them slowly and carefully*.

Figure 17–1 shows one way to choose your reading list, mainly from the books on business and politics that made *The New York Times* best-seller list. If you set such a list as your minimum target to be competitive, it is a doable job.

		Highest Rank on List	Weeks on Best-Seller List
1980	*Crisis Investing,* Casey	1	6
	The Coming Currency Collapse, Smith	7	3
	Free to Choose, Friedman	1	12
	The Third Wave, Toffler	2	6
	Managing in Turbulent Times, Drucker	11	1
	The Real War, Nixon	5	3
	On a Clear Day, General Motors, Wright	10	3
	Sylvia Porter's New Money Book	11	1
1981	*Soul of a New Machine,* Kidder	10	2
	Lord God Made Them All, Herriot	1	8

Figure 17–1 Books on business and politics that made best-sellerdom. (Data from *The New York Times* Book Review)

	Highest Rank on List	Weeks on Best-Seller List
Theory Z, Quel	10	5
Art of Japanese Management, Pascale	13	1
The Alpha Strategy, Pugsley	13	2
Complete Money Market Guide, Donoghue	3	3
Wealth and Poverty, Gilder	7	2
Paper Money, Smith	3	3
1982 *The One Minute Manager*, Blanchard	2	50
Keeping Faith, Carter	5	2
Indecent Exposure, McClintick	5	2
America in Search of Itself, White	6	3
The Fate of the Earth, Schell	3	4
1983 *The Price of Power*, Hersh	5	4
Megatrends, Naisbitt	1	60
Creating Wealth, Allen	4	28
In Search of Excellence, Peters	1	65
Nothing Down, Allen	8	10
1984 *Further Up Organization*, Townsend	9	9
Powerplay, Cunningham	10	10
Iacocca, Iacocca	1	85
1985 *Passion for Excellence*, Peters	1	28
Re-Inventing the Corporation, Naisbitt	7	9
Funny Money, Singer	9	8
1986 *Greed and Glory on Wallstreet*, Auletta	6	13
Ford: Men & Machine, Lacey	5	16
The Reckoning, Halberstam	3	16+

Figure 17–1 Continued.

A book that is number 15 on the best-seller list will sell perhaps 150,000 copies. In the United States, there are a few million executives. So only one of ten of your competitors may have bought a book at the bottom of *The New York Times* list. However, number 1 on the list may have sold a million or two copies (*Megatrends* did about eight million), and thus most of your competitors will have bought the book. So in the past seven years, there are really only about a half-dozen books that the majority of businesspeople have probably tried to read, one per year. If you simply read one book a year, *carefully*, you may be ahead. Who knows how well you might compete if you tried two! One per month and you can be considered an order of magnitude better read.

COMPETITIVE READING II

In any given decade, a few business writers will dominate the best-seller list, as well as the commentary of (lesser) business consultants. These best-selling writers and their books are worth special attention.

The first thing to do with these books is to buy them. Put them in your office. It looks good for you to have them, and you must never underestimate the power of appearances in business and in human affairs of any kind.

The next thing to do with these books is to *examine* them by flipping through them, and maybe reading a few parts here and there that strike your eye. But do not feel guilty about not reading them word for word. Rest assured that they will not work in detail; in other words, their step-by-step methods will not provide magic to your business, or else it would not be necessary for the gurus continually to write new books. To see this, diagram the books by title and author, as shown in Figure 17–2.

The books by leading business consultants, such as those in our diagram, result from the contacts that the consultants have with leading businesspeople, usually CEOs of large companies.

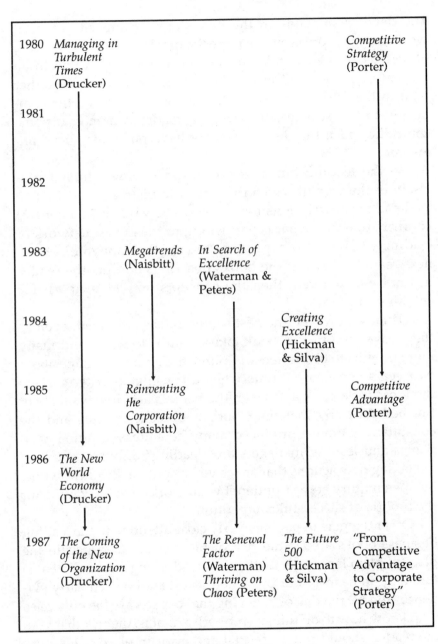

Figure 17-2 Diagramming books by leading business gurus.

The detailed methods in the books are a composite of what works, or more precisely, a composite of what works in the belief of selected CEOs, as told to the consultants. The value to an individual reader will more likely be in certain pieces, rather than in the whole composite. Occasionally, however, the composite works like a gestalt, giving the reader awareness of some controlling idea that he or she may have previously been unaware.

So the leading business books have value, but not precisely in the way in which they seem to be intended—that is, as detailed prescriptions for success. The value is in a general confirmation that what is happening to the gurus' network of leading CEOs is also happening to you, the anonymous business reader, or not. If the books describe concepts the reader has not encountered, then the concepts may be a tip-off for catching up.

Usually, however, the best-selling books are dated, even as they leave the press. A book takes months to write, and many more months to be printed and published. It may average about two years between the time when a consultant-writer garners the ideas for a book and when the book is actually available in finished form. By that time, both the businesspeople and the consultant will have produced many new ideas. Leading companies and leading managers are "leading" only because they are taking new actions that are as yet unwritten. Business works by open inquiry at the frontier of what works, not by waiting for the reports of successful competition.

Other dangers in paying overly close attention to the leading business books are (1) the risk of picking up on jargon in the place of plain language, (2) the risk of adopting a concept that is founded on hearsay but presented as if based on scholarly evidence, and (3) the risk of believing that experts are the only ones who know how to do things "properly," that is, the risk that you, the reader, should put aside trial and error in place of learning first to be an expert.

The story of business is never fully written. The unwritten portion, the unnavigated waters, is where the principal money is being made. When you can read about it, it is old news; when you can research it in scholarly detail, it is ancient history.

There is no management concept so right in theory that there is not more power in its execution, but there may well be management concepts that are more right than what you have got.

USING BOOKS AND BOOKSTORES

The building of intellectual capital requires reading more than best sellers. Each person's intellectual capital has a singular structure, and this structure is continually evolving; when you are on the edge of new growth, which is always, you need fuel for the next leap, and it is not possible to say what type of fuel (what kind of idea) you may need. So you must be committed to "patrolling" for the next idea that fits the open niches in the structure of your intellect.

Let's go back to the fact that some 50,000 books per year are published in the United States, half of which are nonfiction. How many of these appear on the shelves of a bookstore? If you are an inveterate bookstore patroller as I am, you can calculate the number yourself: The nonfiction shelf at a typical mall bookstore is about six feet by six feet, and holds about 500 books, which, allowing for duplicates, means about 250 separate titles. The inventory on the shelf turns only a few times per year, so I would estimate that no more than a thousand different titles appear in the course of a year. This is 1,000 of the 25,000 nonfiction titles, or only 4 percent.

The titles that appear in a bookstore are meant to be the best-selling ones. But while it is important to know about the best sellers, as we have discussed earlier, it is also vitally important to find the next piece to your own intellectual jigsaw puzzle. This piece may not show up automatically; this "missing piece" is not obligated, as by universal law, to show up in the 4 percent of titles on the best-seller shelves.

The next recourse is book reviews, but this avenue is also not an end-all. The most prestigious general review, perhaps, is *The New York Times* "Book Review." In the nonfiction category, there will appear each week about two dozen reviews (including paragraphs and short squibbs), and in a year's time this will amount to about 1,000 titles—and these will be closely correlated with what appears on the shelves of the chain bookstores, which therefore does not help with our puzzle.

Next is the book reviews in trade magazines and special journals, of which there are thousands, each with many reviews per issue—so that in the end, virtually every title of the 25,000 nonfiction books per year actually does get reviewed. But accessing the hundreds of journals that may be required to cover the needs of your particular intellectual juncture is no different than directly accessing the almost innumerable books themselves. It is not possible without a 2,400-hour day.

What these facts and figures begin to suggest is the enormous role of serendipity in the development of intellectual capital. The only option is to patrol as great a number of different bookstores as possible—perhaps building this job into your travel plans.

The freedom to pick up a book, physically and examine it briefly greatly increases the odds of a "find" (compared to reading a review) and greatly reduces the time wasted on "bad finds" (which you may not discover until you actually purchase and start into a book).

The more bookstores and libraries you can find time to try, the better. I never go to a new city on a business trip without finding the best bookstore I can; I see it not as a luxury but as part of my business; I see it as part of being smarter than my competition.

Another good place to patrol is the new bookshelves of major university libraries, and sometimes of good college bookstores. It provides perspective to see what scholars are publishing and reading; it may or may not be appropriate for you to read the books.

Electronic searches, by the way, can be very helpful in finding books to solve a particular problem, but computers cannot be programmed to find what you need to read next, in terms of the broad context of your intellectual life and growth. Only your own real-time patrolling can do it.

So choosing which books to read is a critical job for the intellect, although not one that can be reduced to a codified system. There is simply the scanning of candidate titles, the examining of portions of the book, and the commitment to devote a part of your precious resource of time and energy to some particular, perhaps obscure book that seems somehow to "fit."

Here are a few other brief rules about choosing books that I find helpful:

1. Be careful of books by multiple authors; the best writing flows from one intellect to another; multiple authors have multiple intellects, and they usually have an impossible task of agreeing on what is "true"; the style of multiple authors will often be dull.

2. Also be careful of books that are merely collected *articles* by diverse authors; articles are articles and cannot be melded together into a "book-length idea," which is what you want from a book; if you want to read articles, then read articles (more on this later).

3. Do not buy books that seem to you, upon examination, not to be well written; no matter how much the subject seems to "fit," the element of style has equal weight; substance and form are equal.

4. If you have to force yourself to read a book you have chosen, you have chosen the wrong book. Scrap it and start over with another book; give it away, but do not hold it on a shelf and

let it make you feel guilty about not reading something you "should."

SUBSTITUTING BIBLIOGRAPHIES FOR DISSERTATIONS

A natural urge of the intellect is for complete information and complete understanding. This urge, unconstrained, leads to the desire for a PhD dissertation on every subject of importance to your intellectual life. The urge can be broken, at least temporarily, by a two-pronged approach: (1) philosophical surrender to the existence of an overwhelmingly complicated universe, in which simplification is the only mode of operation, and (2) occasional forays into careful, annotated bibliographies.

The philosophical surrender is the most difficult part. You must recognize that the universe is more complicated than you think it is and that it is more complicated than you can even imagine it to be. Your job, in business, is to adopt simplifications that work better than your competitors'; your job will not usually be helped by exhaustive research, except occasionally in the natural sciences and technology, but rarely, if ever, in the understanding of markets.

The surrender is easier if you occasionally succumb to the desire to cover a subject thoroughly—perhaps some aspect of economics, politics, or history that you do not understand and that keeps appearing in the daily news, nagging at you to upgrade your fluency with it. In such a case, you can wade into the library yourself, electronically or physically or both, or you can employ an expert in library science to do it for you. When you feel that you want to select not simply the most current books but the all-time best ones, the bookstore route, which emphasizes patrolling and serendipity, should be replaced by the good scholarship of someone who knows libraries and who can interview enough subject experts to find both consensus and creativity.

"DARWIN'S NOTEBOOK": PAYING SPECIAL ATTENTION TO IDEAS WITH WHICH YOU DISAGREE

Charles Darwin's book, *Origin of Species* (1859), expounded one of the most powerful ideas of all time. It is said of Darwin's career in science that whenever he came across an opinion (or a report of a fact) with which he disagreed, he gave it an entire page in his notebook—the better to test his own evidence and objectivity.

Following are notes on a book I purchased a while ago because of how vigorously I disagree with its conclusion. The book was *Engines of Creation: Challenges and Choices of the Last Technological Revolution* by K. Eric Drexler.

> *Notes on Drexler.* Drexler is a Research Affiliate at the MIT Space Systems Lab. According to him, we are about to enter a dramatic new era of technological progress. One of the advances will be what he calls *hypertext*—a kind of global information link-up, indexed electronically across all subjects and languages, contributed to by all five billion humans, and accessible via a portable terminal the size of an ordinary textbook of today. The entire world will be a paperless office. Hypertext will allow readers to see whether linked sources support an idea or linked criticisms explode it. This will mean that we can evaluate complex ideas correctly, that we can have "fact forums," that we can proceed without embarrassment from errors, and that our foresight will be greatly strengthened.
>
> My subtitle for this book is, "The Perfectibility of Man Via High Technology." The book set me to wondering, irreverently, how any author could make such an enormous error. The book after all *is* published; it contains 300 pages of English prose; there are hundreds of citations and footnotes. I conclude that:
>
> A. Safely inside a lab at MIT, Drexler does not daily have to test his ideas against a market; and
>
> B. As confirmed by the book's bibliography, Drexler simply has not read widely beyond the literature of science.

What Drexler is missing is *common sense,* that faculty by which we make connections between disciplines and draw conclusions that cannot be drawn from within the disciplines themselves.

A READING PROGRAM TO CAPTURE GLOBAL TRENDS

The significant thing about markets today, for American companies, is that the crucial movements are *global* in nature. If you think you have a trend staked out, and it does not have a global component, you should probably think about returning it to the drawing board. The supreme way to beat competition today is to see how global factors are reaching your own narrow corner of the world.

A good process for capturing global trends was not taught to many of today's leading executives when they were in school. At that time, the domestic economy was still closed; things were much simpler. This is all gone, and the only executives likely to stay afloat are those who dedicate themselves to finding their global linkage. Executives must train their minds to look for the global aspect of every business situation.

The tools for capturing the trends, apart from the mental dedication just mentioned, are shown in Figure 17–3. All researchers and line executives have a set of tools like this. The assortment is important: You need daily, weekly, monthly, quarterly, and annual balance. Trends occur at different paces. Some trends can be stated simply in the newspaper, and others require a book; many global trends require direct experience before they can be consciously registered.

CLIPPINGS

The "how-to" of clippings may seem an inappropriate topic for a chapter on capturing global trends—like pausing in the middle of a supercomputer design manual to discuss how best to solder one wire to the next, and both to a terminal. However, the proper care and selection of clippings is an important general factor in your capacity to apprehend global trends. The confidence you have in your filing system for clippings (and indeed for all paperwork) contributes directly to your perception of new ideas. Furthermore, this confidence bolsters your courage to hold and defend new ideas against objections, which come almost immediately, from within and without, for virtually any idea that is original enough to help you make money.

Stressed in this chapter is the fact that no one can read everything and that no one can remember all of what he or she does read. At any given moment in the intellectual life, only a few strands of thought will be present, and it is not possible consciously to select these from our entire store and command them to come forward for incorporation into bigger and better concepts. The assembly proceeds to a significant degree of its own volition. There is a comfort provided to this process by the standing knowledge that you have collected, extrasomatically, a host of supporting fragments of interesting and potentially helpful news items and other insights.

The clippings that most attract us and that we carefully save for future reference are rarely if ever actually examined again as we may have promised ourselves. But nonetheless, the process of selecting and saving those clippings is somehow essential to what the intellect can do, especially to the span and tenacity of the intellect in search of genuine globalism.

Another function of clippings is to facilitate networking, a subject covered later. You send clippings to other intellects, along with your personal annotations, saying in effect, "This item has been thought-provoking to me, what do you think?" Good responses by other people to the "raw material" of your concepts can have irreplaceable value.

The choice of clippings is similar to the choice of what books to read: you cannot read everything and you have got to choose a precious few. The storage of clippings after you have got them,

Daily Newspapers (read during the morning, slowly)

I prefer *The New York Times* for in-depth coverage of national affairs, politics, business, and advertising; and the *Financial Times* of London for coverage of Europe, Asia, and commodity markets.

Weekly Magazines (read at night)

I prefer *Business Week* for its economic bulletin and for the many case studies of individual companies, and *Time* for its coverage of popular events and possible trends.

Monthly Reports (read during the business day)

I prefer the *Federal Reserve Bulletin* for monetary statistics and topical articles on world money and banking; Morgan Bank's *World Credit Markets* for Euromarkets, and *Scientific American* for news of where technical breakthroughs may occur.

Quarterly Journals (read on the plane)

I prefer *Foreign Affairs* for global politics and economics, and for what big-name bureaucrats are saying, and *Wilson Quarterly*, published by the Smithsonian, for what leading scholars are presently finding of interest outside science.

Books (read on the plane and on weekends)

I find about one every other week that's exciting; my current backlog includes *The Bigness Complex, The Closing of the American Mind*, and *The Leading Edge*.

Selected Reports (usually by government)

I find about one each quarter that's worth reading beyond its executive summary. I look at the data appendices first to see if there are new items—otherwise the report is merely a new interpretation.

Seminars, Conventions, and Trade Shows

There is no substitute for learning directly from others, especially the "leaders" who appear at conferences. I try to attend two per year in my areas of greatest ignorance.

Figure 17–3 Tools in capturing global trends (structure of the author's personal reading program).

Data Sorting and Graphing

There is also no substitute for your own particular brand of "empiricism." If I think I've got a new global trend and can't show it to myself on paper, I know it may not be real.

Private Intelligence Network

Your friends and colleagues are also indispensable. I try to trade "intellectual capital" with someone new at least once a month, to expand my network.

Bellwethers in Everyday Life

New products, new publications, new advertising approaches, and new technologies sometimes first become evident, not in publications or research, but in everyday life.

Figure 17–3 Continued.

however, is a little different than what to do with books because at least it is evident that books go on shelves. Clippings go in subject files, and the creation of the right subject files—not too many, not too few—is an equally important matter to the growth of intellectual capital as selection of individual chunks of raw material in the first place. Creation of subject areas for storage "feeds back" into the selection process for individual items.

It is not possible to say, ahead of your creating them, what subject areas you should have. Likewise, it is not possible to say, in the fashion of a foolproof recipe, what individual items you should cut and save other than to clip the ones that catch your eye.

My own categories and rules for which clippings to save are as follows:

1. I like "Darwin's Notebook" clippings.

2. I do not like clippings of standard economic data; this can always be found when needed in standard economic sources.

3. I like "nonstandard" data, if I think I might need it some day—like the size of a typical orchid farm in Hawaii, which I am sure won't show up in reference books.

4. However, I am not building a reference book or a personal encyclopedia for future use. In time, probably before I need it again, *all* data will indeed be gathered and put in appropriate books and data bases.

5. I sometimes like graphs and tables that interpret data in new ways.

6. I like a clipping on which I feel compelled to write or underline with a bold red pen. I may strongly agree or disagree.

7. I especially strive to save clippings that say to me, "One day you'll want to refer to me, and if you don't save me now, you won't know where—or under what subject—to ever find me again." This is a clipping that is somehow hooked to a concept of which, consciously, I am not yet fully aware.

8. I try not to save items that are primarily tutorial, for such material will also be anthologized and accessible to electronic searches. For example, suppose a journalist writes on how something works, like the stock options market; I may not have understood the subject before reading his or her treatment, but nonetheless I do not save it; I know there are or will be better treatments in books if I am really interested.

9. I usually do not save editorials, at least pure editorials. I like opinions, but only if they simultaneously contain new facts about the world. In *The New York Times*, these are sometimes captioned "News Analysis." In the case of big stories, like the Challenger Explosion or Iran-Contra Affair, such analyses are good shortcuts and time savers. But I know there will be books on the subject quite soon, and I do not save clippings for the sake of competing with books.

10. I like clippings on subjects that standard authorities will regard as offbeat. I know I have got one of these if I feel a little

embarrassed to save it. For example, suppose I am interested in world money and trade, interest rates, exchange rates, the actions of the IMF, the Fed, and the like. I come across a story on the scale of drug trading in Panama; it is lurid, but it talks about billions of dollars of goods and about "laundering the cash" in big banks. I save it. I know that such a story will not be "polite dinner table talk" with bankers or ranking economists, but I nonetheless know that the world works in sordid ways. I want my intellect to function beyond the merely standard approaches.

"Good clippings" suggest their own subject labels. You might go a week, let's say, without forcing subject labels onto a stack of clippings. Then when you sort through them again, they start to break up of their own.

How many clippings should you save? Once again, the natural tendency is to save too many, not too few. Do not appoint or hire a "clipper." It does not work. The result is simply a new burden of guilt, a new reminder that you cannot absorb all the information in the world today. Hiring a clipper (or a clipping service) surrenders the selection process from your own intellect, and this is precisely what you cannot forego.

As you can see from the structure of my own personal reading program, I look at two or three newspapers a day and several magazines per week. Some days there are no new clippings for my files. On other days, there are several—I doubt if I have ever cut more than seven or eight in a single day. So the average might be two or three per day, or about a dozen per week. Not a hundred; you cannot manage it. Not merely one or two, you need to be a little less rigid in your (unwritten) rules of selection. Take on a few more "oddities" and "quirks."

Finally, should clippings be indexed? My answer is no. I have learned that no matter what "index system" I create, simple or elaborate, I soon outgrow it with the passing of time and the accumulation of my intellectual capital. Subject areas fade, they merge, they disappear, and they reappear. The most living part of the intellect is perhaps the "living indexer." If there is a way to compensate for its peculiarities and failings with electronics, the claim I make is that involving the mind in an active, living process of clippings (cutting, taping, assigning subjects, arranging by chronology, etc.) is precisely the answer to "indexing" what you know, how it fits together, and how it will (of itself) produce new combinations.

Global Newspaper

The world has thousands of cities and tens of thousands of newspapers, written in hundreds of languages. But if the world is eventually to become a single "global village" engaged in peaceful commerce, shouldn't there soon be a *global newspaper*? Especially, shouldn't there soon emerge a newspaper for the international *businessperson*, one that treats the economic and political affairs of, let's say, Yugoslavia, in the right proportion with those of, for instance, India, Poland, South Korea, or Brazil—or California and Canada?

I think we might all agree that our own local American papers—mine is the *Toledo Blade*—do not meet this broad requirement. Some people will surely disagree with me, but I would argue that the two leading U. S. business newspapers, *The Wall Street Journal* and *The New York Times* are not global either. It is not that both of these papers do not have great value to American business; certainly they both cover foreign affairs; nonetheless, they simply are not what we can properly call "global."

The closest candidate in the English language (which is the only practical language to consider) is the *Financial Times* of London, now available the same day in most major U. S. cities. I began taking it several years ago, and it took me almost a year to learn to read it (and to like it). To say the least, it is not written in eighth-grade language.

What I find most intriguing is the depth of economics coverage. How different this level of interest and understanding is from what we find here in the United States!

Another very interesting thing is the *relative weight* of stories given by the editors. Examine Figure 17–4, which shows how the same news item was treated by the three different papers. Only

	The New York Times	The Wall Street Journal	The Financial Times
Location	Front Page	Page 3	Page 6
Headline	GAUGE OF ECONOMY SHOWS THIRD DROP IN 5-MONTH PERIOD	Leading Index Declined 0.1% In September	U.S. leading indicators remain static
Subhead 1	Further Slowing Seen	Basically Flat Trend Seen As Sign That Softening of Growth Will Go On	
Subhead 2	But Few Analysts View 0.1% Fall in September as Sign Recession Is Imminent		
Subhead 3	The decline in the leading indicators is the third in the last five months.		
Length	28 column-inches	18 column-inches	6 column-inches
Chart	Yes	Yes	No

Figure 17–4 Three treatments of one story, November 2, 1988.

the *Financial Times* put this story in proper, global perspective; both *The Wall Street Journal* and especially *The New York Times* felt obliged to create a big story where not even a small one really existed. In other words, American journalists insist that every indicator, every month, must *mean* something; it must be a story; this is silly. The *Financial Times* buried it on page 6, where it belonged, because the European journalist could see that, in the present month, it meant little.

Sometime when you see the *Financial Times* at a newsstand— it is peach colored and a little larger than American papers— pick one up as an experiment. You will appreciate (1) how much more complicated the world is than you were hoping, and (2) how much more sophisticated the European world view is than the American view.

18

Building a World-Class Network

NETWORKS PROVIDE INTELLECTUAL CAPITAL EXCHANGE

Ideas form within a single human intellect. A committee does not have an idea, as a committee; some single member of the committee has the idea and brings it forth for comment and elaboration. A committee does not produce ideas unless at least one of its members is an "idea person"—and even then the risk is that the committee will be more of a wet blanket than an enabler of ideas.

But even though ideation is a singular mental process, the human intellect benefits from exchange with other minds; in fact, there is probably no greater influence on the mental life than the inputs, objections, and criticisms of other people. Early in our lives, we form networks with other human beings who help structure our intellectual capital: First comes family, second comes friends, and next comes colleagues in school, in university, and in business. They are all part of our network.

What I want to discuss here is the value of a conscious and deliberate extension of one's network beyond the normal scope of family, friends, and colleagues; an extension whose purpose

189

is to reality-test one's most precious ideas and points of view, and to risk doing this with other intellects known to you as "world class." For example, in the middle of my life (in 1981), I am employed in the American grain export business, and the industry is facing a second embargo against the Soviets over their possible behavior in Poland. My job is to advise grain traders on what is likely to happen and how to *watch it unfold more surely than the competition.* What I need is not only the latest data on grain shipments but the best possible insight on international politics and on the history of Soviet behavior in similar situations. Will they invade Poland and squash the Solidarity Union, or will they find another way to maintain control? Millions of dollars of grain shipments are at stake. How can I achieve "world class" global ideas about this situation?

I am caught without a network on the subject; I do not personally know any of the ranking experts on Soviet affairs; and as I read up on their scholarship, I am struck by the fact that few if any of these traditional Soviet experts know anything about the particulars of the grain business. I determine that mutual education will be required; I need to learn about the Soviets and global politics, and they about grain exports. Somehow I recognize that the *leading* experts will not be interested in my problem, except in exchange for large consulting fees. I make a map of the university resources around me in a 75-mile radius, and interview a half-dozen professors in Soviet studies. I assemble them into a "foreign affairs panel," for a modest fee, and put questions to them directly from the trading floor. I moderate the panel, and translate their answers into plain language the traders can understand. It helps. I start to learn about Soviet affairs.

Over the course of the next months and years, one member of the "panel" becomes more and more interested in the details of the grain industry, and he begins to apply his lifetime of study toward it, and he and I together begin to have new ideas that seem to us "world class." We have new ways to quantify what the Soviets must spend to import grain versus what they must first earn from the sales of their own gold, diamonds, oil, and natural gas. We write these ideas up and begin to exchange them with the "ranking" experts. Gradually these experts are added to our network. They are interested in us because we have new intellectual capital to trade with them. They do not require consulting fees, in cash, but they do require intellectual capital; but it is a fair trade. This is an example of the deliberate extension of networks beyond their beginning points of family, friends, and business colleagues.

The university is a good spot for extended networking, but by no means the only one. There is also the state and federal government, whose bureaucrats need exchanges with businesspeople to reality-test their own proposed initiatives. A fruitful place to "lobby" is at the analyst level of government, as opposed to the ranking official (i.e., the elected senator or representative); it is not exactly "lobbying"; it is exchanging ideas. The government analyst has ideas about how to design or administer a program; he or she wants to know how it will work; he or she wants to trade intellectual capital with someone in business who will listen rather than harp about "free markets." The businessperson who understands the need to test ideas before implementation can certainly out-network his or her competition. The key to networking with government analysts, as with university professors, is to *read* their material carefully and to prepare your own careful analysis in response, and to offer your position humbly, in clear spoken or written form.

There are other sources of networking besides university and government; in fact, there are unlimited sources. There are professional organizations, community service groups, and the clergy. For senior executives, there are leadership in national associations and election to the boards of other companies; board memberships may, in fact, be the ultimate network for CEOs. There is no substitute for comparing ideas with someone who is "in the same boat."

If you are less than a CEO at the moment—let's say that you are just beginning to build intellectual networks—keep in mind that your target should be "world-class" minds in the subjects of greatest pertinence to you. Be prepared to build slowly. Be prepared to earn the privilege of trading intellectual capital with them. First, you must have ideas that you can document and publish, perhaps more locally than nationally or internationally, before expanding the network. It may seem odd, but the best route to global breadth is a narrow niche. Concentrate on the small part of business that you know about the best, express it clearly, and attempt to frame it globally, but do not attempt to "globalize." Stay in your best, narrow niche, and let your growing network expand you.

These are the tools of networking:

1. Packs of clippings with your personalized annotations ("preprocessed raw materials"). Keep in mind that *very few* people, professors included, read widely, especially not *The New York Times* or the *Financial Times* of London. Sending them selected items can be of real value.

2. Correspondence. Everyone likes to be taken seriously. I have found no better way to begin a new network than to write a long, careful letter to an author whose book or article I have liked; this is particularly true of works in the scholarly or academic press, but it also works with best sellers; people may give well-known authors acclaim, but this is not the same as giving them new ideas.

3. Publications or newsletters. There has to be a regular vehicle for you to express your own ideas, so that others are free to read them. Personal correspondence tends to stay personal, but a newsletter can be circulated without permission among a wide variety of people, which serves as an introduction.

FUTURE OF NETWORKS

Some time ago, a friend of mine who had lost his high-ranking corporate position due to a restructuring, and who was still hunting for a job, said to me, "Boy, I've learned one thing—I need a better *network*! I'll never again just concentrate on the people in one company. The only thing that matters in my situation now is how big my network is."

In the same vein, another acquaintance told me that when you are job hunting, your network acts as your marketing department. "Not your sales department," he said, "but your marketing department. Your network will tell you who you are and what you really have to offer and it will also suggest avenues of inquiry, people and companies and types of needs you could satisfy, but it won't actually close a sale for you."

The concept of a personal network is something we all pretty well understand. It is not a new or revolutionary idea. As my father used to say, in the days before computers and electronic linkages, "It's not what you know but *who* you know."

And indeed, *electronic* connection between people, in and of itself, is not what is important. The electronics are secondary. The key thing about connections and networks is the flow of intellectual capital, and your own understanding of its nature.

In June of 1989, *The New York Times* carried an article by business professor Ralph Kilmann of Pittsburgh called, "Tomorrow's Company Won't Have Walls." Kilmann says that in the twenty-first century, companies will have adopted a *network* form of organization. The companies will own fewer actual physical assets and they will work by a global array of human resources that enters into many overlapping joint ventures, partnerships, associations, informal cooperation agreements, consortiums, and temporary deals. This network style of organization will stretch today's traditional definition of where one company ends and another begins.

I agree with Kilmann on the likelihood of this development, but I do not agree with him on what it will look like *inside* the network, if that term can even be used. Kilmann says that each network will have a *hub*. "The hub of the organization," he says, "will be comprised of a small staff that will be responsible for the strategic and management focus of the company. It will set priorities and company standards, and it will work out ways to motivate the other members of the company."

I see two errors in the idea of a hub of a network: (1) The best networks, virtually by definition, cannot *be* controlled or managed. They cannot be given a sharp focus; and (2) even more importantly, no network lasts if some so-called hub must provide motivation. (I am not talking about reward, which is something that the market, and only the market, provides.)

Management professors, in their concentration on monetary capital rather than intellectual capital, have long misunderstood *motivation*. Motives are not something that comes from outside a person, but from within. Motives are not created out of thin air by managers (as to fit a strategic plan) and given to workers; motives are something that resides, spontaneously, within a worker—waiting to be tapped.

I suppose that in a sense we are each the "center" of our own network. But we are not its hub, the way that Pittsburgh is a hub for USAir. Information does not have to travel first to us and then back out in order to reach its destination. Information can flow around the edges of our network without touching us; information can go freely from any one node of the network to another. In fact, information is only attracted to the "center" if what we do to it is not to control it but to amplify and enrich it, and send it on.

A central characteristic of intellectual capital is that you receive more of it if you concentrate on giving it away. You will be a better "center" of your network if you think of yourself not as a generator but as a conduit.

From a commercial standpoint, the center of a network organization will not provide motivation. Instead it will recognize the special motivation and talent which already exists (at given nodes), and then perceive patterns into which this can be woven to fit niches in the marketplace, niches which the network itself has helped the center to see. The center of a network organization will work better the less it is an elite commander and the more it is a humble superconductor.

SPEECHMAKING

The pursuit of reason in disorderly situations is aided by the careful use of language. Better decisions are reached when a group is clear about what is happening. The difficulty in business, however, is that most discussions are informal, take place between colleagues who know each other, and rely on special language or jargon, whose meaning is never explicitly questioned.

One way to test your reasoning is to give outside speeches. Having to give a speech before an audience forces you to structure your ideas and to attempt to say them clearly and plainly. Audience feedback tells you how well you have done. It is like a very inexpensive "test market." The damage you may sustain is not likely to be monetary but rather to pride and ego, altogether a little less painful way to accumulate intellectual capital.

It is not possible to give a speech on some highly specific, perhaps confidential business initiative. But it will usually be possible to give a speech on the general area from which the initiative derives. For instance, suppose you have invented a new consumer product, "A." You cannot give a speech on "A," without tipping the competition. But you might be able to give a speech on "Consumer Product Trends," in which you test the basics of your position. Someone in the audience may say, "Consumers are fed up with new cheap products, and want better quality," or "Consumers want leisure time products, not appliances," etc., challenging your overall framework, especially if "A," known only to you, was a low-cost toaster.

Businesspeople often complain about giving speeches as an unprofitable waste of time. I would agree not to go overboard. But the complaint is mainly about "stagefright," the age-old

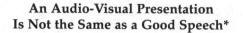

**An Audio-Visual Presentation
Is Not the Same as a Good Speech***

- "Dot Lists" don't help when you have nothing significant to say

- "Dot Lists" insult the audience when you *do* have something significant to say—if you can *say* it well

- All lists, whether on the screen or on paper give the illusion that you know how the points are connected—this is usually not true, and this is why you should attempt to make the connections come alive in coherent prose

- Concepts which *require* graphs cannot be carried away by the audience in a form they can use, namely in words

---

*Advice from a former A-V addict.

Figure 18–1

pain involved in putting yourself in front of people in such a way as to let them judge your ideas, their substance, and their clarity. But this *is* business, putting your ideas in front of people for them to buy.

Giving speeches not only test-flies your ideas, but also may expand your network; in each audience there will be two or three people interested in the same niche and struggling with the same world view as you. Often they will come forward after your talk, identify themselves, ask questions, and indeed seek to become a part of your network in the future.

———19———

Adding Life to Business Strategy and Research

WHERE DO WE GET VISION?

Management consultants have been preaching the value of a "corporate vision" for nearly a decade. The successful CEO is one who not only has the right vision, but also who can communicate it, simply and powerfully, so that a big organization can understand it and follow the score. (The unsuccessful CEO appears on the cover of *Business Week*, as James Robinson III of American Express did in mid-1990, under the headline, "The Failed Vision.")

Business books say a number of things about vision, but they really do not tell you how to produce it. The books talk about imagination and foresight, and about helping people to understand the broad situation being faced, and sometimes about the applicability of poetic language and eloquence. But there is no patented ten-step method that leads to an appropriate business or political vision, as if from a pop-up toaster. Good business vision is something you have, or it is something that comes to you, almost willy-nilly. Some consultants claim they can create, via special group processes, favorable conditions for the emergence of a corporate vision, but the good ones acknowledge that they cannot guarantee this.

One thing that does not regularly produce a powerful vision is an abundance of facts and details. This is not to say that an executive can do without the facts, but that the true leader must somehow reach beyond them. Computers, in particular, are virtually sightless when it comes to successful future plans.

Reaching Beyond Science?

At one level, all of us seem to know perfectly well what is meant by vision. We awake and our eyes see the morning sunrise; this is vision, at its simplest, ocular level. Scientists tell us that rays of light impinge on the retina, causing images to form that are transmitted to the brain for processing. A simple case of bioelectronics. Operational flaws in the physiological system are corrected by laser surgery.

Can it really be so simplistic? We are each a computer chip atop a camcorder?

Before modern science, up through and including Leonardo, most thinkers believed differently than scientists today, that, in fact, visual perception was the result of an act of the soul outwards, that the visual image is not formed passively on the retina but rather is synthesized by the human judgmental faculty.

Nonsense? Maybe so, and certainly, as I said, not scientific. But how different is this ancient conception of vision from what we say we want from our political and business leaders?

When we demand "vision," what do we really expect? We know that the future cannot be accurately foretold, but is this what we want anyway, someone who can do it? Or do we merely want fresh words and a better understanding? (In this case, will the trend continue, as in Czechoslovakia, of electing recognized artists to the highest political office?)

Courage and Risk

I think that what we really want in a person of vision is indeed a glimpse of his or her soul, a feeling for the fire within—in this regard I suppose I agree with Leonardo about vision. When it occurs, it reaches beyond the facts (beyond "intelligent foresight") and beyond the routine methods of science. Political and business vision involves risk and requires courage. The creation of more value from less requires a design for "seeing ahead" to what *might work*, though it has never been tried.

There will always be an enormous demand for people who have such vision, and no doubt also a surplus of (wrong) explanations for how they do it.

MUST WE DEVELOP A "MASTER STRATEGY"?

In business, we like to think that competence reigns supreme. But the law of insufficient competence contradicts this. Each of us, including the company's CEO, is always short some amount of competence for the job we are in—or else the firm for which we work is uncompetitive. We each need to form additional intellectual capital to ascend the scale of relative competence and bring success to the firm.

But success is founded on the ability to learn from failure. Therefore, the firm must have an outlook that enables trial and error rather than an implicit rule of "success without failure." The outlook that most endangers learning is the one that says, "We have a *master strategy*, and the team (like soldiers) will now execute it." The outlook that most enables learning is the one that says, "We have a plan, but it can be changed as events require. The future cannot be predicted. We don't know for sure what will work before trying it. We must proceed in an unending, *open inquiry*. We are always testing, never finalizing."

When an outlook of open inquiry is present, the emphasis is away from "experts who have right answers before something is tried." When open inquiry is present there is less pain in failure because trial and error is genuinely expected. When open inquiry is present, criticism (scholarly, "literary" criticism) is sought by all because it contributes to learning and to the odds for success on the next try.

A key ingredient of open inquiry is humility—or what a colleague of mine calls "The Big 'H'." The trap to avoid is the myth of business, perhaps embedded in a newly earned title (e.g., manager of operations, or vice president of marketing), that a person has reached a position where the knowledge that got him or her there will keep him or her there, without the potential pain of new trial and error, and the formation of an ever greater stock of intellectual capital.

SHOULD WE STAND FOR A LITTLE "CHAOS"?

Late in 1987, two books were published with the word "chaos" in the title: *Thriving on Chaos*, by Tom Peters, the well-known management consultant and author of business books, and *Chaos*, by James Gleick, a science reporter for *The New York Times*. But the embroilment of businesspeople in chaos has been known for a long time, well before these two books—one telling the businessperson to enjoy and to "create" chaos, and the other telling us that while the universe is chaotic at heart, a new science is emerging to grapple with it.

The relevance of chaos to business is just this: There is more potential profit in bringing order to a condition of high disorder than there is in bringing order to a condition of low disorder.

A competent businessperson is one who has learned the ability to swim in chaos without bringing it to intellectual order too soon. In other words, the longer you can put up with a disorderly (and apparently chaotic) situation, before deciding on an approach to order it, the better your chances for profit. But of course, if you wait too long, a competitor may beat you to the punch. So yet another dimension of competence is the talent for living with a complex, hectic situation (or market, or initiative of any kind) long enough for a higher order solution to come forth, but not too long to lose out to someone else (even though he or she may have a lower order solution).

The emergence of a science of chaos is comforting. It gives confidence that even "complete chaos" has order to it if you look hard enough and long enough. I recommend Gleick's book on the science of chaos because most businesspeople have had college mathematics courses in which the crucial assumption was made *not* to deal with any function that was not "well behaved." The math teacher will have refused, for instance, to treat a graph or curve in which there was a sharp discontinuity or gap, and yet the businessperson will find such conditions in market reality, immediately upon graduation. After many years, however, mathematicians are finding ways to deal with "catastrophes" and other seemingly chaotic events, without merely calling them "random." The underlying principle that all of humankind's affairs, the "well behaved" and the "not well behaved," can be treated by reason—at least to some small degree—is important to business. It confirms the role of building intellectual capital and of beating the competition by coming a tiny fraction closer to truth than it does.

DO WE NEED CONSULTANTS?

The average consulting fee in the late 1980s was about $1,500 per day. Beginners charged $500, and some Harvard professors required $4,000, plus lots of advance notice to squeeze clients into their schedule. The demand for capable consultants in the 1990s continues to outstrip the supply. Billings are said to be growing at 15 percent per year. Are consultants really worth all this money, or are businesspeople being fooled?

Let us first consider the broad context of American business today and the changes it has seen since World War II. The best

--- ◆ ---

Charm

To put your ideas into action, to put them on trial, requires the approval of others: bosses, bankers, regulators, and so on. To obtain such approval requires a number of human traits, such as persuasiveness, enthusiasm, dedication, and many others, all of which can best be summarized under the label of "charm."

In his convincing book about the American entanglement in Viet Nam, *Backfire*, historian Loren Baritz says:

> The higher one rises in a bureaucracy, the more impor-
> tant charm becomes, because the more important the
> bosses of the boss are, the more they are "generalists,"
> the less they know, and the more they must rely on
> charm as an instrument of manipulation. Indeed, if one
> really goes high enough, the major questions of the
> board of directors, of the electorate itself, are questions
> of personality. Charm is the response to such questions.
> (p. 333)

What Baritz is indicating is that there comes a time in the life of (good) ideas when they will no longer stand purely on their own merit; the world is full of (good) ideas and people in power, bosses, know this. Experienced bosses have heard hundreds of (good) ideas before and they are calloused to sales pitches on any idea's rational merits. Competition forces the idea's author to develop more than just the idea itself, but also to possess the *charm* to get it through the bureaucracy.

An idea itself, if it exists in a "raw" form as ideation, really cannot be separated from whether or not it is saleable. Presentation is as important as substance. An idea that is very complicated may not be saleable because it is too difficult to communicate, time after time, as must often be done in the course of large bureaucracies. According to Baritz, this was part of Kissinger's problem with regard to Viet Nam and other foreign-policy issues. Kissinger had a grasp of global linkage well beyond his peers; he could see the interconnectedness of many dozens of issues; but his colleagues and the hundreds and thousands of others who were needed to execute Kissinger's ideas could not always grasp the large concepts involved. Big ideas are not always communicable.

known change over this period is the shift toward a "service economy." This shift is very well publicized and is often cited by worried futurists as evidence of an unsustainable movement to a "fast-food" economy, in which no genuine industry remains and in which we are all consuming each other's services. Some of this worry may be well founded, but it is mostly an exaggeration. Much of the shift is more a matter of accounting than substance.

In the 1950s, American corporations did everything for themselves. Corporations prided themselves on having a wide array of complete "service" departments: a complete accounting department, a complete advertising department, a complete PR department, and so on. As time passed and competition intensified for the American market and as the overhead costs of maintaining full-time professionals grew (due to health insurance and other benefits), companies began slimming down. Services were cut from large corporate rolls and service people were released. But it turns out that the need for these services did not go away. In fact, just the opposite is true; the need for accounting grew with every new government tax program; the need for advertising grew with every year of more intense competition on national television, and so on. So what happened is that the corporations hired the people back that they had shed, but in the form of independent services with lower overheads. On the books of our National Income and Product Accounts, this was all counted as service, not as manufacturing.

The result of these trends is this: If you find yourself believing today that you ought to be able to do everything with "in-

— ✧ —

"Epistemological Auditor"
New Corporate Position

Epistemology is the division of philosophy that investigates the nature and origin of knowledge. An epistemologist is one who is concerned with the right structure of your knowledge, including the right structure of your knowledge of business. The existence of "rightness" can be detected by a generalist; in other words, no field of knowledge is so specialized that it has unique principles of organization and truth; in fact, just the opposite is true. A narrow discipline will be found to have a "right structure" that has many elements in common with all the other disciplines in humankind's collection.

Businesspeople have difficulty knowing what to do next. No matter how much knowledge they have of their business, and how many times they have tried their ideas against the reality of their markets, they are still never completely sure what will work best the next time. Often, the CEO of a business employs a staff to assist him or her in the unending task of assessing the market and deciding what to do next. The next move is then based on "everyone's best knowledge."

A CEO who seeks the truth about his or her markets and who also seeks a true assessment of the strengths and weaknesses of his or her own company could be said in other words to seek the Right Structure of his or her Business Knowledge. Such an executive faces a twofold problem in achieving rightness: (1) Every person, businessperson or not, has trouble distinguishing between the way he or she wants things to be and the way things are; and (2) leaders have a need to display optimism about the future, not just realism (truth).

One resource that all executives should use, and that most certainly do, is an *epistemological auditor*. In plain language, this is "someone to check your thinking." It is not an employee of the firm in question. Many times it is the same as a friend, especially a friend in some other field of business, or even not in business at all—someone who knows you well and does not address you as "Mr. President." It is someone who has no stake either in wanting things to be as you want them or in maintaining your optimism.

A company's board of directors could be thought of as the ultimate auditors of the CEO's thinking. The concept of board members paid to check your thinking may be useful: No matter what your present rank in business, or in life, if you do not presently have an epistemological auditor, appoint one. If necessary, pay him or her, but as an independent consultant, not a full-time staff person. The single intellect has extreme difficulty perceiving and maintaining a fix on truth; another mind, especially one with experience in a branch of knowledge separate from your own, can see the flaws in your structure of thought and can help you to a higher degree of rightness.

---

house" resources, you may not be facing up to the true competitive picture. Your competitors are hiring more and more experts on the outside. If you expect to treat business situations with as much competence as they do, you should consider hiring the same class of expertise as your competitors do. In other words, the "normal" or "average" company today, because it has become "lean and mean," is not likely to be staffed for the full range of problems and opportunities it will face. Such a company will not be accruing a truly exceptional cost by hiring consultants because most of its competitors will already be doing it too.

But are consultants really *experts*? And if so, how do they get that way?

Common sense tells us that there are really only two ways to do something new, or to do something old better: (1) Do it yourself, via trial and error or (2) have someone teach you, who has already done the trial and error. It should go without saying that someone who has the experience to do something will not show you how to do it for free. Generally speaking, if it will profit you $100 to learn to do something, it will cost you $50 to learn by trial and error, and a consultant will charge you about

$25. That is how it works. You and the consultant can both make out; instead of the $50 being lost to trial and error (in the face of competition), the $50 is gained at a cost of $25 to you (in the form of a $25 billing by a knowledgeable consultant).

Another way to say this is that consultants are affordable "at the margin." If a new business opportunity (or a solution to an old business problem) is thought to be worth $1,000,000, then existing managers will probably secure $750,000 of this by themselves, without expert advice. But this may leave $250,000 on the table. An expenditure of $25,000 to $50,000 on consulting may greatly improve the chance of making the additional $250,000. This is particularly true when the situation calls for existing managers to participate in new markets or to take old products into new distribution channels.

The way in which a consultant can become an expert is built into business itself, and can be seen once again from common sense. The more you do something, the better you become at it, provided you have the basic abilities, education, experience, and attitudes to begin with. In other words, a chief executive may handle a particular situation only once or twice a year. A successful consultant may be called on to help handle the same kind of situation dozens of times in the same period, and gets the benefit of closely watching how a great many different teams handle the problem. The consultant, in other words, gets "more times at bat" sooner, against a particular kind of pitcher. The extent that the consultant can extract the principles that lead to successful handling of the situation and the extent that he or she can find ways to explain the principles to others and convince them of the potential value of the methods, determines how much he or she is potentially worth to the next client.

The successful consultant must also break the myth that "star hitters need no batting practice." The client must become willing to pay for "practice and warm-up," so that the consultant can perform research and can prestudy each new situation with care.

HOW FAR CAN WE TRUST
"MARKET RESEARCH"?

Market research went, during the late 1980s, literally on trial. In 1988, the consumer products company, Beecham, Inc., began suing the market research firm of Yankelovich, Skelly & White for something that might be called "market research malpractice." Beecham claimed $25 million in damages from Yankelovich because a Beecham product did not penetrate the market as forecast by Yankelovich.

My first reaction to this legal news was sheer disbelief. But the case was real. Beecham paid $75,000 for a market research study of a cold-water wash product called "Delicare," which it intended to launch against market leader Woolite. Yankelovich conducted simulated tests of Delicare and advised Beecham, in a 75-page report, that Delicare would surpass Woolite and achieve a 45 to 52 percent market share, provided Delicare was given the proper advertising support. Beecham launched Delicare, but the new product captured barely a 25 percent market share. Beecham then sued Yankelovich for negligence, misrepresentation, and breach of contract.

Yankelovich denied the charges. Yankelovich said that Beecham provided bad information to begin with, ran different kinds of commercials from those advised, and terminated the ad campaign too soon.

As I say, hearing about this case left me nonplussed. Is Beecham serious? Don't they know that forecasts are often, if not always, wrong? Don't they know that over 90 percent of new products fail, no matter what the research says? What happened to the concept of "Let the buyer beware"? Is the Beecham law department trying to defend its budget?

Upon reflection, however, I found a way to take Beecham's side. Notice that Yankelovich, in 75 pages, predicted a market share figure for Delicare of "45 to 52 percent." This range could be stated as "48.5 +/- 3.5 percent." Doesn't the length of the report and the presumed precision of its conclusion beg for attack? What market research firm does not also know the facts about product failure (nine out of ten), and what market research firm does not know that *it has no power to predict the future to plus or minus 3.5 percent*? So is not Yankelovich guilty, at least, of carrying out the typical charade of most market research, the pretense that markets can actually be plumbed in advance with "scientific" methods?

What should Beecham do in the future? Abandon all research? What should Yankelovich do? Give a range of 10 to 70 percent? What, in other words, is the proper role of research in business?

To answer this question, we must first divide up "business" into a few component parts. I will address the general question of research's role in business by answering three separate questions:

1. What is the role of research in the technical aspects of product development?

2. What is the role of research in the decision-making aspects of marketing and marketing management?

3. What is the role of research in the enhancement of the creative aspects of marketing (especially of product promotion and advertising)?

In the development of material products and technologies, where scientific experiment is truly possible, it seems clear what the role of research should be. The R&D lab is to apply scientific principles to come up with new products never before conceived. In the case in which a product has been invented outside the R&D lab, the lab (again by application of the scientific method) is to find ways to improve it, or at least, get it past government regulations and other market hazards. So with technical research, the question is not so much what the role is, but how much should be done? Top management of a company such as Beecham typically answers the question about how much

R&D to do by means of "proof of the pudding"; in other words, over a period of years, management judges the track record of technical research and determines whether it should be expanded or collapsed, aimed at different classes of products, and so forth. The decisions are not easy, but they are blessed with a little more "tangibility" than other kinds of "soft" research.

The second question is much more difficult for most companies to answer and the third even more so. What is the role of research in the decision-making aspects of marketing and management? Can research help in the selection of what products to bring to market, how to do it, and what to expect from an advertising investment?

My own answer is this: Market research does not relieve the decision-maker of the burden of the rightness of his or her decision. Market research does not substitute for sheer marketing competence. The role of market research is to help make decisions more rational; it makes the factors in the decision more accessible by large teams of managers.

In a business situation, managers are all operating from bits and pieces of knowledge. The job of research is to go back for all the facts and assemble them, on the premise that this may cause new insight and illumination. In concept, this is not much different than the function of an explicit "pro and con list," suggested by Benjamin Franklin in 1772. All of us, including our most talented marketers, make better decisions not from pure intuition but by the exposure of our intuitive ideas to rationality.

The third and final question concerns the role of research in the enhancement of promotional creativity. Here, in my view, research is follower rather than leader. Creativity is in the lead. A small amount of formal research may help a creative manager be more creative, but research will never prove the case, scientifically. The only test that matters is the test of the market. The market, in its complex reality, cannot be simulated ahead of time. But pieces of a final puzzle can be tested. Research that can be done quickly and cheaply, in time to keep up with the product team, can sometimes help. But the team judges this, not the researcher.

HOW MUCH SHOULD "SCIENTIFIC RESEARCH" COST?

The first thing that many businesses assume about scientific research is that bigness—laboratories, equipment, staff, and thus money—is a requisite for "breakthroughs," especially in the realm referred to as basic research. Recent history does not support this—in fact, perhaps just the opposite. Large corporate research labs may do more to discourage than to harness scientific creativity. And large universities, with their built-in disposition to seek grand theory as opposed to niche improvements, also do not enable the best single human minds to soar.

The second assumption is often that advances must be made here, in America, in order to benefit the country most. This too is questionable. The job of (American) business, as it goes on restructuring to meet the market, is to acquire and apply the *best* R&D, regardless of its source, and to incorporate it into its products more rapidly and surely than its competitors.

Furthermore, and at the very heart of the reality of the 1990s, is the fact that R&D resources supposedly cut by corporate raiders have not actually disappeared into thin air. The creative work force still exists and is still functioning, and its new entrepreneurial format is no doubt growing rather than diminishing. We should not be surprised that measurements of it fail; national indicators have always missed significant changes in trends and in the rerouting of resources.

What is presently being tested is the idea that bigness is needed for basic breakthroughs, as opposed to the following:

1. Direct contact by scientists with the market.

2. Better rewards for successful output.

3. Intellectual freedom from bureaucratic rigidity.

The only thing I find distressing about the alarm over American decline is the alarm itself and its source. What we have is a lack of confidence in America's real function in the world: to liberate the individual, to permit individuals to serve the market with what works, and to draw on and mix all of the world's cultures. At the very moment that other countries in the world are rediscovering this, our own politicians, bureaucrats, and university deans are urging the opposite approach: more bigness, more centralized wisdom, more planning and control, and, in essence, more protection for their existing large (but unproductive) facilities. Their handwringing is not so much alarming as simply tiresome. The underlying forces of business will ignore it and go for what works.

IS THERE A "BEST METHOD" OF RESEARCH?

No method is so powerful that it reveals all. In fact, every revelation, by its own power, *conceals* some other part of the picture from us. While we are fascinated by what we do see, there will always be unseen but mighty forces quietly at work altering the whole world. These assertions follow from my claim that the universe is more complicated than we think it is, indeed more complicated than we can imagine it to be, and diversifying further every moment.

Consider a few of the methods that trap even the most famous of global trend-finders:

1. In *Megatrends*, John Naisbitt says that his main method has been the reading of vast numbers of community newspapers, searching for "bellwethers." A bellwether is a ram that leads a flock of sheep. When you see such a ram, you may (normally) expect a flock to follow. But, of course, not every ram will be found with a flock; and many flocks will turn subtly on their own, exerting a "follower-to-leader" pressure. *Note:* The main appeal of *Megatrends* was the title word itself, "mega-

trends." We are all convinced that such things must exist. But in my view, it is a false hope that the world can be simplified into a handful of discrete propositions called trends or megatrends. The world is simply not obligated to do this. It need not kneel to human intelligence. And to believe that you can come to possess "master ideas" may blind you to what you can do, which is barely to outdistance your competitors (in the nick of time).

2. Professors of all kinds are trapped by the concept of tenure, which in turn relates to the practice of "publish or perish," which in turn upholds the peer review process and the dominance of journals that will only publish findings that can be supported by "empirical science." New ideas, bereft of elaborate supporting data, do not flourish in academia.

3. Historians are trapped by the wealth of detail provided by millenia of evidence and by the need to make history "readable," that is, to tell a *story*. History itself is not obligated to move according to the structure of lively narrative.

4. Novelists not only like stories, they also like drama and rich characterization. Human affairs can be dull and boring, yet nonetheless real.

5. Harvard Business School is blessed by and trapped with the case study method. Students apply themselves to dozens, if not hundreds, of cases. But in studying details, the intellect begs for theory. Not all theory is necessarily bad.

6. Business researchers, including myself, are often trapped by what will work to make money, with small teams of people, over short periods of time. This is not necessarily what will assure the long-term survival of a firm, nor is it what may be the best source of guidance for government policy.

7. Of all the traps mentioned so far, none is more perilous than the so-called "science of economics." Economists confine themselves to phenomena that can be measured and to theoretical methods that can be mathematicized. The world, in the

framework of economics, is seen as a giant Swiss watch, and the economist's quest is for the keystone by which fine-tuning can be achieved. Strict adherence to economics blinds the intellect to at least one-half of all human affairs. Humankind is dually rational and emotional; politics relies as much on unquantifiable emotion as rational and quantifiable "laws" of supply and demand. Economics cannot be ignored, but it cannot be the queen of your intellectual approach.

How do we avoid the traps? The only solution is what wise people have always called "independent thought," the main tenets of which we are attempting to develop afresh in the present book.

MULTIPLE PATHWAYS AND OCKHAM'S RAZOR

You cannot do all the things that have been suggested in this chapter, certainly not at once, and perhaps not ever. We all have the appetite, however, to fill up our plate with more than we can handle. We have the feeling that if we follow all the good-sounding methods we hear, we will achieve perfect knowledge.

Let me close the chapter with two master principles that, upon first examination, may seem contradictory. (In college days, a friend told me that he had concluded that the world was built of paradoxes. Today I think maybe he is right, maybe not. But I am sure that the world-class business intellect must have complete tolerance for *concepts* of the world that are paradoxical. We must not be put off by contradiction. It occurs so often.)

Multiple Pathways

In slang, this principle is called, "There's more than one way to skin a cat." The important point, however, is that nature (the universe) really believes in this principle; nature, for instance, did not invent merely one kind of cat but dozens; not one kind of dog, but dozens; not one race of humans, but dozens. When you see rain begin to strike a dry pavement and the streams of water begin to flow, do the streams all go in one narrow, geometric pathway? No, nature prefers multiple pathways.

The message of this principle to the intellect in search of global trends is this: Forget master strokes, forget home runs, forget elegance. Find a bunch of small things that work. People, like nature, prefer multiple pathways.

Form versus Content

When you are advancing an idea and begin to feel resistance, that is precisely the moment when even greater intellectual capital can be created. You must see that dimension of business called "approval" as an inherent component of the idea you are selling; you must be prepared to sacrifice what may seem like critical elements of the "pure idea" for the sake of getting to try the idea, or at least a shadow of the idea. Most of the times in my life when this has happened, it has improved things.

Those with an intellect active enough to be interested in a book such as this usually err on the side of overly elaborate ideas, when simpler ones would do. So the bureaucratic process that forces simplicity and the use of charm can be defended as saving us from more than a few elaborate "backfires."

A good test for overcomplexity is the written word. If you cannot express the idea in clear, plain language, if it requires elaborate charts, mathematics, and jargon, then it will probably have difficulty in the boardroom. The bosses and their bosses become ever more generalist and spend ever less time on a multitude of tough details.

Ockham's Razor ("The Principle of Parsimony")

The way that William of Ockham, 1343, explained this principle is that "plurality is not to be assumed without necessity. . . . What can be done with fewer assumptions is done in vain with more." Nothing is to be assumed as necessary in accounting for a fact or situation unless it is established by evident experience or evident reasoning.

The message of this principle for me has always been *ruthlessly* to cut my list of what to do. The *Razor* reinforces the drive toward simplification; the mind, especially the academic mind, wants to enumerate and re-enumerate, to complicate and recomplicate; but nothing happens unless we simplify. We must surrender avenues of thought that are beautiful and precious to us, but that are nonproductive. Nothing so disinflates my guilt over a less-than-dissertation-length treatment than to recall Ockham and to ruthlessly wield the *Razor* to my sprouting intellect.

—20—

A Single Suggestion about Computers

"OVER MY DEAD BODY"

One of the best and most challenging jobs I've ever had was a consulting project to assist an agency of the U.S. government in making its research findings easier to understand by the typical, everyday user. The assignment went on for two years, and the agency's principal editor and I developed new methods that worked, we thought, much better than the old ways, methods that we began calling "user-friendly." The key to these methods was the use of certain desktop publishing software, then available mainly on the Macintosh computer.

The executive head of the agency was pleased with the results and asked me to come to his quarterly staff meeting to give a summary briefing to him and his managers. At the end of my presentation (which took place in early 1990), the chief executive asked me what I would recommend he do to insure that the new user-friendly methods become a permanent capability of the agency and that they become as widely used as possible by all the researchers and the editorial staff.

"The easiest thing would be to put a couple of Macintosh computers down in the publications section," I replied. I knew

216

that the agency had previously standardized on IBM-compatible computers, but I thought that top management would have little objection to a couple of "Macs" in the building for this special purpose.

There was a long silence in the room after my suggestion, and then the chief executive said, "I don't think we can do that because two years ago we standardized on IBMs. Isn't there some way we can do these things on IBM?"

"Not at the present time," I said. The chief executive looked dubious and resentful, and I chose not to argue the point any further. A few days later I was told in confidence that, upon my exit from the briefing room, the agency's data processing manager had said to the chief executive concerning my suggestion for putting Macs in the building, "Over my dead body!"

Although I will not be able to escape referring to it entirely, the purpose of this chapter is not to debate which personal computer is best, the Macintosh or the IBM. Instead, the purpose is to dig into the underlying and exceedingly ticklish issue of why chief executive officers (and many other levels of executives too, but I will refer throughout to the CEO) have remained by and large "computer illiterate," and at the same time why data processing managers have not by and large tapped into the enormous new resources available in desktop software today, whether Mac-based or (now) IBM-based.

"COMPUTER LITERACY"

It will no doubt come as a great relief to the CEO reading this that I will not be recommending that he or she become "computer literate," certainly not in the sense that this phrase has come to mean. But neither will I say that the CEO can and should forget about personal computers.

In fact, just the opposite. My recommendation is that today's CEO must become "Windows literate," and the sooner the better. If this seems equally frightening, my advice is, "Relax. A very pleasant and important surprise is waiting for you!" And furthermore, "You can test my thesis privately, without getting the whole organization exercised."

It turns out that the personal computer has actually been invented twice—the first time with an operating system called MS-DOS, and the second time with an operating system called Microsoft Windows. This is something of an oversimplification, of course, inasmuch as the Macintosh began life (in the mid-1980s) complete with its own version of Windows.

But the essential point is this: If your main experience with personal computers has been with the industry standard machine (an IBM-compatible device, relying on an Intel 286 microchip and the MS-DOS operating system), you are like a person who has had to learn an entire, demanding new language from scratch ("C-colon-backslash," etc.) and who is understandably not anxious to repeat the experience. And if you never actually took time to learn the DOS language (i.e., you did not become "computer literate"), you may be thinking that an "advanced" language like Windows will be even worse, or that you will probably be required (finally) to master DOS before you can move on to Windows. It turns out, however, and very happily, that Windows is free-standing. Knowing DOS is like having taken Latin in high school—an instructive experience, but only in a mainly academic way, and certainly in no sense a prerequisite for full command of everyday English.

If what I say is true, then why all the heat? Why does the hair on the neck of many corporate data processing managers stand on end at the mention either of Macintosh or Microsoft Windows? And why do so many CEOs stand back from this argument as though it is just too tough to crack? Most of the answer lies in the sequence of events by which microcomputers entered the American workplace. Let us briefly review this history, before going on to the future and to what I consider the enormous potential gains in intellectual capital awaiting the CEO and his or her firm from a whole new look at personal computers in the 1990s.

BEFORE WINDOWS

The 1970s, as we all remember, was the decade of the mainframe computer, a technological innovation that forever changed company record keeping, accounting, and operations of all kinds. In the early 1980s, personal computers arrived, and most big companies welcomed the eventual entry of IBM, whose name and reputation they trusted from the mainframe sector. The conviction was that IBM would provide leadership and an umbrella of uniformity that everyone could rely on.

The early IBM PCs, and somewhat later their clones, were equipped with the Microsoft DOS operating system, and all of the early PCs were touted as being "user-friendly." This claim may have been true in a literal sense, but only in comparison to what had gone before. In other words, the DOS commands were no doubt "friendly" if your only previous choice was to learn a full programming language used on mainframes, such as FOR-TRAN, BASIC, or PASCAL.

But learning DOS well enough to do much beyond simple word processing and spreadsheet manipulation proved to be much more difficult for the average worker than the IBM marketers (and other so-called "computer types" or "techies") had imagined. Companies that invested in early PC hardware, with a view to adding efficiency to office routines and to raising the long-term productivity of their work force, saw a very small gain, most of which was eaten up by the cost of "supporting" the machines and of training the users. A company with a few dozen PCs required two or three (or more) full-time technicians to keep the machines running, to connect them to printers and other auxiliary devices, and to install and update the burgeoning number of new (and not always compatible) software application programs.

One cost-control method or efficiency secret that the entire PC industry recommended and that corporate data processing departments liked was networking. Most DP professionals had their roots in the operation and care of mainframe computers, and the electronic networking of PCs seemed to them a very logical extension of previous practices. Enormous expenditures were made to link and lock-step all the new PCs, on the grounds that this approach would save money and simultaneously improve productivity and communication within the organization. The result, in retrospect, was disappointing, to say the least. But the investment has been made and remains in place. The idea of having to do it all over again, now in the cost-cutting decade of the 1990s, is enough to make any CEO dubious and resentful.

Meanwhile, the fact was missed by DP professionals and CEOs alike that Apple's Macintosh, which had been launched in the mid-1980s, actually did have a user interface that really was friendly. The main reason that the Macintosh was overlooked by "serious" corporate users was that its files were not easily compatible with IBM PCs or with the older IBM mainframes. The compatibility issue, as we can see now, was greatly overrated, as today's technology permits virtually any kind of file translation, quickly, from one platform to the other.

SINCE WINDOWS

As the decade of the 1990s opened, and with tens of millions of standard PCs in place throughout the country and the world— 80 percent of which use the MS-DOS operating system—the Microsoft Corporation began delivering its new system called Windows. Macintosh users called Windows a "complete copy" of what they felt had made the Mac the Mac. Indeed, Apple Corporation sued Microsoft (and Hewlett Packard) for several billion dollars for infringement of copyright, a suit that has proceeded now for several years and that Apple appears to have lost.

Quite apart from the legal issue, Windows has made Microsoft the king of all high-tech companies in the world, perhaps even surpassing IBM in the market valuation of its outstanding stock. The reason, as mentioned earlier, is that the personal computer is being invented a second time. Not by IBM this time, but by Microsoft's Windows. All the millions of machines out there, configured with DOS, are obsolete. Not so much in terms of the hardware, which can in many cases be inexpensively upgraded, but in terms of the operating software. The stock market knows that, over the next few years, Microsoft has tens of millions of orders for Windows built in. The breakthrough in "user-friendliness" is so great, it is literally worth tens of billions of dollars.

COMPLETE REASSESSMENT

"Okay, okay, I get the point," the CEO reading this might say by now. "I'll have my data processing manager take a fresh look at the situation and decide whether we should do something."

If the message of this chapter has been ticklish already, here is where the going gets really tough. The reassessment of personal computers is not something the CEO should delegate, but something in which he or she should participate directly.

The reader will keep in mind that my perspective on this subject is in terms of intellectual capital. I am not speaking either as an experienced CEO or a long-time data processing manager. However, having made my living for several years by means of the personal computer, I see something—in the new profusion of dramatically powerful, Windows-guided software—that the CEO should experience firsthand. My recommendation may not work for every CEO who tries it, but I am sure that it will work for some if not for most.

"Okay, okay, I'll run down to the computer store today," the potential convert might say, mainly in jest. "But what am I trying to do? Do you want me to learn how to type my own memos, keep my own appointments schedule, do my own accounting, or what?"

I would be very pleased, of course, to elicit this sort of response from anyone in my target audience. The answer I have in mind is specific, but probably not in the way the inquirer will have imagined. I do not have much interest in convincing a CEO to type memos, keep schedules, or do accounting—this to me is all a very secondary issue. I have a much grander agenda involving the interaction of the CEO's intellect with today's powerful desktop software. This is an interaction that essentially cannot be delegated, because only the CEO has the CEO's mind. Only the CEO knows the company's numbers in terms of the forces driving them and the human capabilities for improving them.

Returning to the first part of the question, however, let me quickly endorse the idea of "running down to the computer store today." This is exactly the thing to do! Surely an experiment costing a few thousand dollars is not out of line with what could come of it.

HUDSON 1–2–3

Here's what I think the "non-computer-literate" CEO should do:

1. Purchase one of the new notebook-sized computers. The brand is no longer a key factor, although if the choice is an IBM-compatible machine (a so-called "386" or "486"), it must have Microsoft Windows. (Few sales are made without Windows these days, but be sure that Windows is installed and running before leaving the store.) If the choice is Macintosh, go ahead and get the top of the line, the PowerBook 180. (The Macintosh System 7.0 should also be installed before you leave the store.) Budget: Not to exceed $5,000, including an inexpensive, portable (or semiportable) printer ($500).

2. Purchase a spreadsheet for the Windows software package, such as Excel or Lotus, in addition to whatever software might come with the machine. (Don't argue much with the salesperson about which software is best and about the question, "What do you want to do with it?" Most salespeople don't use the software, they just sell it. They will not generally understand

that you are conducting an experiment.) Later, by magazine or catalog, purchase lots of other software, including an organization chart maker for Windows program. Budget: Eventually, $2,000.

3. Find a seminar to attend for a half-day or so in which software company representatives demonstrate their packages on a big screen in front of a large audience. It really doesn't matter which software packages—the ones you have or others; what you want to see are the eventual possibilities and "how easy it looks." (It "looks easy" because it is easy, once you acquire the knack for closing all the manuals and letting Windows do the work. This is one of the things that I feel most strongly that CEOs must see and feel for themselves, because it will affect their entire perception of what their organizations can eventually do with the new technology.) Budget: $1,000 or so, including the trip.

Before the advent of computers in the late 1960s, I worked for the CEO of a small manufacturing firm in Ohio. We all regarded the boss as the "ultimate tightwad." Our travel expense forms consistently came back with questions and pointers for saving money. But one day as he and I drove downtown together for lunch, the CEO asked me if I ever stopped in at the office supply store next door to the restaurant and "just browsed around." He said that he recommended forming this habit because he had found that you will occasionally discover things you did not know about that would help you become better organized and that it would be worth the money. Coming from the "ultimate tightwad," the boss who insisted we submit minute-by-minute trip plans before he would approve tickets, this suggestion to "browse" in an office supply store struck me as absolutely shocking, though, of course, I gradually discovered that he was absolutely correct. I still have the habit today of shopping for better tools, without a specific predesigned list.

No doubt my three-part ($10,000) recommendation will seem "shocking" to some executives, because of the business myth that "competent managers plan everything ahead."

There is really no way to "browse through" the capabilities of the present generation of personal computers without owning one, and thus my 1–2–3 recommendation above. By the way, for the CEO undertaking my experiment, I specifically recommend the notebook-sized computer, not the desktop-sized one. The portability is part of the experiment, and these days the manufacturers are packing all the new technological power into the notebooks, more so than the desktops. The notebooks may be called "toys" by a DP manager, but in most of the corporate office buildings I enter, my PowerBook 180 will turn out to be the most powerful PC on the premises.

INCREASING THE
FIRM'S COMPETITIVENESS

Now back to the goal of this game. What I want the CEO to do is, first, to play with the performance numbers of the business, and second, to play with the organization, the two things he or she knows more intimately than any other person alive. I want the CEO to get good enough with a Windows spreadsheet and organization chart maker to be able to think with them. I want the CEO to be in direct contact with the numbers on the screen, without having to ask human subordinates to do the manipulating for him or her. I am betting that the changes the CEO can make to the format (alone) of the company's numbers will be worth the whole effort. The same value will accrue, I believe, from the CEO's direct, onscreen analysis of organization structure, new product and market potentialities, economic and sales projections, new concept communications, and many other subjects.

The final question to deal with is, "What lies ahead for the firm if the CEO's experiment is successful? Will this process lead inevitably down the path of (re)investing $10,000 for every employee?

To begin answering this, at least in part, let me return to the issue of compatibility, which was brought up earlier in my brief history of the business use of microcomputers. The compatibility issue—setting aside the recent advent of powerful translation software—still contains most of the remaining emotional heat in the personal computer question, and certainly most of the potential cost of reinvestment. But the "heat" is not so much a computer issue as a business strategy issue: Will the company gain competitive advantage in the 1990s from further workplace standardization or from a new emphasis on innovation? This is the really powerful reason why the CEO must be involved personally in the reassessment.

The electrical connection of "personal computers" into fully compatible networks (with or without Windows and other advanced software) is the equivalent of changing them into "work stations." No company has enough money to equip itself with uniform stations that are advanced enough for its most able and creative employees, without "wasting capacity" on the average user. Electronic schemes to "serve" the network with different levels of software capability may work, from a purely technical standpoint, but such schemes inherently require the same high-cost technical support as before, with the early MS-DOS networks. Should the question not be raised if this cost can be avoided? Has the technology and the software not progressed to the point where much less central support is required? From a reliability point of view, are not the new machines more like typewriters and copy machines than what we used to think of as computers, with an occasional call to a serviceperson being required, but not a team of full-time technicians?

And furthermore, if the grand goal is full compatibility for all machines in a company, who can actually make the analysis ahead of time of where to start or what to buy first? The advances are coming too rapidly, for one thing, and the avenues that any given type of software might open up for a company cannot, even in principle, be predetermined.

CONNECTIVITY

In questioning the value of electronic networking, I may have led the reader to think I recommend nothing beyond a collage of free-standing, independently configured machines. Not so. My intent is to break the myth that every corporate use of PCs must be via networks. As I said, this costs lots of money, tends to "gridlock" creativity, and quickly falls behind regular advances in the industry.

But the question should surely be asked, "Will that little notebook computer be able to talk with the company's main-frame?" The answer is, "Yes, certainly, with the proper modem and software."

But connecting to mainframes will not prove to be a make-or-break-issue. It will not be a prerequisite to enhanced creativity and innovation. And besides, most companies today already download aggregated data on customers, operations, and finance into a PC spreadsheet like Lotus for further (more user-friendly) analysis. This is the point at which the CEO will plug in, initially by diskette, maybe later by modem. The contributions I expect the CEO to make in form and substance will be at this "top layer" of analysis; they will not affect the mainframe operations at all, unless, of course, it is determined that the "right" information is not in the company computers to begin with. And a discovery about the inadequacy of records could hardly be considered a "computer glitch"; it is more of a major strategic event.

PROPER STATE OF MIND

As mentioned earlier, I am not advocating that CEOs undertake "Hudson 1–2–3" in order to be able to type their own memos, arrange their own schedule, or keep the books for their own administrative profit center. In addition, I fully recognize that the demands on the CEOs' time are overflowing and that when the CEOs are fully engaged in making important decisions, the skills they need are not computer-centered, but people-centered. In the midst of a busy day of meetings and daily emergencies, CEOs will not generally be tempted to play with Windows on their notebook computers.

But my overall presumption here is that the CEO spends some small part of his or her life (maybe evenings, weekends, on airplanes, in hotels, etc.) reading, writing, and thinking about business. In this state of mind, the CEO will be excited to discover what the reinvention of computers can mean for enhancing his or her own intellectual capital, and in turn that of the entire corporation.

Summary

The goal of this book has been to suggest effective ways of building intellectual capital. What I mean by "intellectual capital" is the combination of:

1. Your genetic inheritance.

2. Your education.

3. Your experience.

4. Your attitudes about life and business.

Of these four factors, the one you can do the most about in mid-career is your attitudes about life and business.

An individual's intellectual capital is singular in structure. No other individual has the same quantity and quality. But the definition of an individual's intellectual capital can hardly stand apart from three other factors that characterize the organization of which the individual is a part:

5. Systems.

6. Culture.

7. Research.

The goal of building more intellectual capital is to beat the competition and increase the profits and longevity of the company in question. The goal is not to reach truth, in the absolute, but to come minutely closer than competition, and sooner.

We live in an age of enormous material abundance, due to our special knowledge of science, engineering, and technology, and due to the continuing emergence of political freedom all across the earth. The world is becoming more and more complex. We have a surplus of information, but a shortage of knowledge, especially of general knowledge or "right thinking" about what human culture should do next.

One of our cultural myths is to revere experts of all kinds. We believe that someone, somewhere understands the world in all its detail and that our individual world view is amateurish. But such world experts do not really exist, as can readily be seen in the incomprehensibility of their writings and the incalcitrance of many problems, such as poverty and hunger. There is no choice but to accept our own world view as preeminent and to make it more powerful than the competition's.

The individual intellect is a prisoner of language, culture, and science. We have inherited the view that nature is a large, predictable "system" and that human society is an economic subsystem of nature, moving in regular, forecastable rhythms and capable of improvement through "systems engineering" (i.e., central control). The big job of the intellect is to burst through language, culture, and science to independent thought. A key attitude is irreverence.

The relativity of truth, the impossibility of predicting the future, and the ever increasing diversity of the universe and markets lead to the concept of a "business *niche*." A business niche is only partially defined by means of economic, political, demographic, and technical parameters, and by the array of monetary capital put against it by a particular company. The key element to success in the niche is the structure of the CEO's intellectual capital and the potential of the niche to enhance it, and vice versa.

Knowledge and money are closely related, but more simultaneously than sequentially. A large amount of knowledge does

229

not guarantee a large amount of profit. Knowledge must lead to adding value to the universe of a kind and at a time when it is really "needed." Profit is created at the precise moment when we do something successfully that we were not sure how to do, or when we do something of common knowledge at the right time.

Because of the risk of failure in each attempt to add value, business and stress are inherently connected. Stress cannot be eliminated, but it can be reduced. The key is often the right set of attitudes. Attitudes can be called the "transmission fluid" in the elements making up intellectual capital.

The only real test of an idea, in business, is not its novelty or its complexity or the credentials of its creator, but whether or not it *works*. The only way to increase overall business competence is to put your ideas to the test over and over again, to fail often, to learn, and to try still again.

The pain of mistakes cannot be avoided, but the pain can be fashioned into better ideas the more you exert a quality, or attitude, of intellectual honesty. This quality that allows you to have confidence through humility rather than the majesty of your organizational position, or that allows you to accept the weight of evidence when it goes against your most cherished position, or which makes you able to talk in plain, clear language, especially about your own motives, when all around you there is obfuscation and hidden agendas.

The intellect is subject to various, powerful "controlling ideas" that govern your behavior until they lead to serious errors. The most useful tools for helping the intellect to break through erroneous positions are "everyday ideas" about getting organized, managing your workload, delegating, speechmaking, imperfectionism, optimism, and so forth. But there is also a host of ideas for finding global trends that can help, such as competitive reading, properly using books and bookstores, selecting clippings, networking, and wielding "Ockham's Razor."

Two aspects of the approach recommended in this book go directly against established business practice: (1) Replacing the "master strategy" fallacy with *open inquiry*, which enables genuine trial and error, and (2) taking an entirely new approach to forecasting, with emphasis on the CEO's ownership of his or her own eclectic outlook, in place of traditional economic models.

The approach requires a new corporate position, that of "Epistemological Auditor." This person is employed directly by the CEO specifically to challenge, often irreverently, the soundness of the CEO's outlook and actions. The auditor is both a generalist and an outsider; if an auditor is brought inside the firm, as staff, his or her independence is broken, and the efficacy of the position is lost.

The enhancement of intellectual capital confers not power itself but the potential to capture power. No idea has value separate from its acceptance or the ability and willingness of the firm to execute it. The effective executive must not only have ideas but the ability to get the ideas sold; this requires clear presentation and the group of traits we call "charm."

Business ideas in the 1990s will be based less on "efficient production (of something) for a profit" and more on the solution to large societal problems. Entrepreneurs of the 1990s will be those who apply their business intellect to the Great Issues, not as advocates but as creative problem solvers.

Bibliography

Baritz, Loren. *Backfire, A History of How American Culture Led Us Into Vietnam and Made Us Fight the Way We Did*. New York: William Morrow, 1985.

Bell, Daniel. The Cultural Wars, American Intellectual Life, 1965–1992, *Wilson Quarterly*, Summer 1992, pp. 74–107.

Bloom, Allan David. *The Closing of the American Mind*. New York: Simon and Schuster, 1987.

Braudel, Fernand. *Civilization and Capitalism, 15th–18th Century*. Vol. 1: *The Structures of Everyday Life, The Limits of the Possible*. Great Britain: William Collins Sons & Co. Ltd., and New York: Harper & Row, 1981, First Perennial Library edition, 1985.

Braudel, Fernand. *Civilization and Capitalism, 15th–18th Century*. Vol. II: *The Identity of France, People and Production*. Great Britain: William Collins Sons and Co. Ltd., 1990; reprint ed., New York: Harper Collins, 1990.

Braudel, Fernand. *Civilization and Capitalism, 15th–18th Century*. Vol. III: *The Perspective of the World*. Great Britain: William Collins Sons and Co. Ltd., and New York: Harper & Row, 1984, First Perennial Library edition, 1986.

Cunningham, Mary. *Powerplay: What Really Happened at Bendix*. New York: Linden Press/Simon & Schuster, 1984.

Dyson, Freeman J. *Infinite in All Directions*. New York: Harper & Row, 1988.

Eliot, T. S. *On Poetry and Poets*. New York: The Noonday Press, 1974.

Feiwal, George R. *The Intellectual Capital of Michal Kalecki: A Study in Economic Theory and Policy.* Knoxville: The University of Tennessee Press, 1975.

Foukal, Peter V. "The Variable Sun." *Scientific American,* February 1990, pp. 34–41.

Harrison, G. B. *Shakespeare, The Complete Works.* New York: Harcourt, Brace, 1952.

Hirsch, Jr., E. D. *Cultural Literacy; What Every American Needs to Know.* Boston: Houghton Mifflin, 1978.

International Bank for Reconstruction and Development. The World Bank, *World Development Report, 1988.* New York: Oxford University Press, 1988.

Jaynes, Julian. *The Origin of Consciousness in the Breakdown of the Bicameral Mind.* Boston: Houghton Mifflin, 1976.

Johnson, Thomas H. *The Complete Poems of Emily Dickinson.* Boston: Little, Brown, 1960.

Jones, Philip D., and Wigley, Tom M. L., "Global Warming Trends," *Scientific American,* August 1990, pp. 84–91.

Kahn, Herman. *The Coming Boom; Economic, Political and Social.* New York: Simon & Schuster, 1982.

Kennedy, Paul. *The Rise and Fall of the Great Power, Economic Change and Military Conflict from 1500 to 2000.* New York: Random House, 1987.

Meadows, Dana, et al. *The Limits to Growth.* New York: Signet, 1972.

Naisbitt, John. *Megatrends.* New York: Warner Books, 1982.

Naisbitt, John, and Aburdene, Patricia. *Reinventing the Corporation: Transforming Your Job and Your Company for the New Information Society.* New York: Warner Books, 1985.

Novak, Michael. *The Spirit of Democratic Capitalism.* New York: Simon & Schuster, 1982.

Peters, Thomas J. *Thriving on Chaos: Handbook for a Management Revolution.* New York: Random House, 1987.

Peters, Thomas J., and Waterman, Jr., Robert H. *In Search of Excellence: Lessons from America's Best-run Companies.* New York: Harper & Row, 1982.

Plato's Phaedo. Translated by F. J. Church. New York: The Liberal Arts Press, 1951, reprinted, 1954.

Postman, Neil. *Amusing Ourselves to Death: Public Discourse in the Age of Show Business.* New York: Viking, 1985.

Schultz, Theodore W. *Investing in People: The Economics of Population Quality.* Berkeley and Los Angeles, CA: University of California, 1981.

Simon, Julian L. *The Ultimate Resource.* Princeton: Princeton University Press, 1981.

Simon, Julian, and Kahn, Herman. *The Resourceful Earth; A Response to Global 2000.* Oxford, England: Basil Blackwell, 1984.

Singer, Max. *Passage to a Human World.* Indianapolis: Hudson Institute, 1987.

Stewart, Thomas A., "Brainpower," *Fortune,* June 3, 1991, pp. 44–60.

Twain, Mark. *The Adventures of Huckleberry Finn.* Philadelphia: Courage Books, 1990.

Twain, Mark. *The Adventures of Tom Sawyer* (1st ed.). New York: A Tom Doherty Associates Book, 1986.

Waterman, Robert. *The Renewal Factor: How the Best Get and Keep the Competitive Edge.* New York: Bantam, 1987.

Index

E

D

F

S

T

V

W

Y